D1391950

Published by BBC Books,
a division of BBC Enterprises Limited,
Woodlands, 80 Wood Lane, London W12 0TT
First published 1989

Dad's Army television scripts © Jimmy Perry and David Croft
This book © Paul Ableman 1989

Designed by Hammond Hammond

Illustrations by Toula Antonakos, Chris Lloyd and Larry Ronstadt

ISBN 0 563 20850 3

Set in 12½/13½pt Sabon
Printed and bound in Great Britain by
Butler & Tanner Ltd, Frome, Somerset
Cover printed by Belmont Press Ltd, Northampton

PICTURE CREDITS

pages 16 left (background) & 18 top & right Imperial War Museum; 20 top
& bottom Robert Opie Collection; 28 top & bottom (backgrounds) Imperial
War Museum; 30 Hulton Picture Company; 33 left Imperial War Museum,
right John Frost Historical Newspapers; 46 (background) Imperial War
Museum; 52 Pictorial Press; 53, 56 (background) & 58 Imperial War Museum;
63 top Brian Hayes, bottom John Frost Historical Newspapers; 67 Imperial
War Museum; 70 E.T. Archive; 76 middle John Frost Historical Newspapers;
80 right Imperial War Museum; 83 left John Frost Historical Newspapers,
right Hulton Picture Company; 90 left Max Rosher, Pinewood Studios (British
Film Year exhibition), right & 99 John Frost Historical Newspapers; 106, 113
bottom & main picture 114 Imperial War Museum.

All other material reproduced BBC ©

DAD'S ARMY
THE DEFENCE OF A
FRONT LINE ENGLISH VILLAGE

EDITED BY ARTHUR WILSON M.A.

WRITTEN BY PAUL ABLEMAN, AND
BASED ON THE BBC TELEVISION SERIES BY
JIMMY PERRY AND DAVID CROFT

BBC

PREFACE

❖ ⟨ ⟨ ◆ ⟩ ⟩ ❖

THE STARTING POINT for this little book is a personal connection with the 'front-line English village' of its title – namely, Walmington-on-Sea in Sussex. Although I visited it for the first time only relatively recently, I have known about it almost since infancy. It was, in fact, the home of the uncle after whom I was named and whom, many people have said, I strongly resemble in both appearance and manner.

My uncle was, in a small way, the 'black sheep' of our family, and a source of some fascination to me. Instead of going into one of our traditional pursuits – government, the diplomatic service, the 'groves of academe' and so on – Uncle Arthur was perfectly content to be a humble village bank clerk. I often tried to picture him there, going about his placid daily round, untroubled by great affairs of state or the responsibilities of high office, and wondered if he had been satisfied with his homely choice. My reflections on this intriguing relative, whom I had never met, were fed by reading the large store of letters which he sent to my father (the two were very close) throughout his lifetime and which my father kept in a large tin box. (I hasten to add that I sought my father's permission before reading them.) When I was ap-

MANY PEOPLE COMMENTED ON THE MARKED RESEMBLANCE BETWEEN MYSELF AS I AM NOW (LEFT) AND MY UNCLE ARTHUR AS HE WAS DURING THE WAR YEARS (RIGHT).

proached by a well-known publishing house to produce a book to commemorate the fiftieth anniversary of the outbreak of the Second World War, it was to Uncle Arthur that my thoughts turned. I recalled that he had been a sergeant in the local Home Guard at Walmington and I decided to pay a visit to the village on the off-chance that it might supply a little material.

It was a providential decision and set me on the trail of one of the most remarkable bibliographical discoveries ever made: a cache of documents and photographs, old newspaper clippings, letters and postcards – a veritable treasure trove of memorabilia. This hoard had come to light just a few months before, during the long-overdue rebuilding of the bank in which my relative had toiled so obscurely. In a section of the cellar, behind a heap of rubble where a wall had collapsed, a great stack of steel document boxes was found. They housed a collection amassed by one George Mainwaring, who had been the manager of the branch as well as the commanding officer of the Walmington Home Guard platoon. The centrepiece was Mainwaring's own wartime log, a work which I immediately recognised as being of unique importance in revealing, with great immediacy and vitality, the day-by-day life of a Home Guard commander in the Second World War.

For a social historian such as myself, it was a veritable Aladdin's cave. I knew at once that this was a book which I had been destined to edit. I promptly moved into the White Hart in Walmington and, for the next two years, devoted myself to cataloguing Mainwaring's collection and filling in the gaps.

My task was made a little easier by one chance discovery: a member of Mainwaring's platoon was still alive and living in Alice Springs, Australia. This man, Frank Pike, whom Mainwaring regularly refers to in his log as 'stupid boy', had, after the death of his 'mum' and his 'Uncle Arthur' (I fancy my relative, although legally unmarried, may not have lacked female companionship entirely), accepted an assisted passage to Australia (the assistance coming from his surviving relatives) and wound up as a toy manufacturer specialising in large cuddly stuffed kangaroos. I flew to Australia and spent a total of 37 hours in conversation with Mr Pike whose tape-recorded reminiscences add another dimension of immediacy to the enthralling story. In terms of intellectual development and general knowledge, Pike had hardly changed from the youth we meet in the Mainwaring Dossier. His reminiscences were rather garbled, since his memory had almost totally

TO PROMOTE PATRIOTIC FEELING, MAINWARING HIMSELF DESIGNED HIS STRIKING BANK MAN-AGER'S OUTFIT.

KEY TO 'THE MAINWARING LINE'

1. Perimeter Defence consisting of subterranean electric railway, surface gun emplacements and other defensive installations.

2. Submarine section of perimeter defence. In addition to installations mentioned in (1) above, this section includes periscopes (3) for discreet surveillance of marine approaches and mines (4) with which to sink incoming enemy aircraft.

5. Electric railway. Until electrification is completed a hand-cranked railcar may be used. (It would be inadvisable for veterans such as Pte Godfrey or Corporal Jones to crank the railcar.)

6. Underground supply dumps.

7. Underground hospital.

8. Marine defence training area (formerly Peter Pan Boating Pond).

9. Anti-tank defences (until installation of concrete 'dragons' teeth' upturned boats from the Peter Pan Boating Pond can be used).

10. Camouflaged sea surveillance point (old Punch and Judy tent).

11. During times of crisis, relays of children on sand can camouflage true purpose of tent from enemy assault craft. They should laugh and clap.

12. Broken pier. (Various uses can be envisaged for this installation.)

13. Railhead. Trains bringing reinforcements and vital supplies will arrive here and the spur line (14) will serve to supply subterranean perimeter fortifications and also to evacuate battle-weary troops for leave, situation permitting. Note brake-men (15) controlling descent of supply wagon (16).

17. Command HQ. (Also church.) Note fortified Lewis Gun position in Church Tower.

18. Alternative Command HQ for use during bank opening hours. (Also bank.) Note semaphore signalling station on roof, chiefly envisaged as back-up for field telephone communications network if we ever get field telephones.

THE MAINWARING LINE
THIS MAJESTIC CONCEPT, DEVISED BY MAINWARING FOR THE DEFENCE OF HIS BELOVED HOME VILLAGE, WAS NEVER ACTUALLY BUILT. VERY POSSIBLY THE BOLDNESS AND ORIGINALITY OF THE DESIGN WERE SIMPLY TOO ADVANCED FOR THE CON-

19. Fortified Communications Hub. (Telephone box.) Note carrier pigeon back-up alighting on roof.

20. Bastion 1. (Formerly Novelty Rock Emporium.)

21. Bastion 2. (Formerly Godfrey's Cottage.)

22. Underground NAAFI.

23. Medical Supplies Depot. (Formerly Timothy White's, the chemists.)

24. Recreation centre. (Formerly Ann's Pantry Tea Rooms.)

25. Assembly points. (Formerly Cpl Jones' Butchers Shop, the Sweet Shop and Frazer's undertaking establishment.)

26. Anti-conflagration centre. (Formerly Fire Station.)

27. Bus station.

28. Centrally situated communications node (old Wishing Elm) with despatch rider's transport (bike) leaning against it.

29. Subterranean Interrogation Centre beneath reassuring Olde Worlde cottage. Note interrogation of senior German officer proceeding below ground while above ground a carrier pigeon waits to take valuable information direct to Whitehall.

30. Defensive trench. (Old drainage ditch.)

31. Sea mine.

32. Land mine.

33. Coastal defence patrol being vetted by periscope.

34. Assembly point and reinforcement depot. (Church hall.)

35. Manned Defensive Positions.

SERVATIVE MILITARY ESTABLISHMENT OF THE DAY. MORE THAN ANY OTHER ITEM IN THE MAINWARING DOSSIER, HOWEVER, THIS DRAWING REVEALS THAT THE COMMANDER OF THE WALMINGTON-ON-SEA HOME GUARD PLATOON WAS NOT ONLY A GALLANT OFFICER BUT A TACTICIAN OF GENIUS.

PETER PAN BOATING POND

failed him, but they have nonetheless proved useful in filling a gap or two left by my other souces.

I should make clear at the outset that the 'Mainwaring Dossier', as I have, in a scholarly paper printed in a specialist journal, named the store of documents unearthed at Walmington, is very rich, and will provide material for research and study for many years to come. The complete log of Captain Mainwaring, for example, would require many volumes. The present work is essentially a sample of the rich feast, containing a mere four entries from the great log out of a total of 420 (including the post-war ones). As for the rest of the 'Dossier', it has been possible to find space for only a small fraction of it. For all that, I am confident that there emerges a vivid picture of a front-line English village in wartime.

IN ADDITION TO HIS SHARP COCKNEY WIT, PRIVATE WALKER WAS ALSO A GREAT ONE FOR PRACTICAL JOKES.

For me it has been an exacting, moving, at times hilarious and yet, considering my family connection with Uncle Arthur, a slightly unearthly experience to produce this book. For the reader, coming for the first time upon the events of wartime life in Walmington-on-Sea, its contents may well seem, in the robust words of Private Walker, who was the jester in Captain Mainwaring's platoon, 'bloody amazing'.

WHAT FOLLOWS IS the very first entry made by Captain Mainwaring in his great log. I have decided to print this because it is clearly of major historical importance and also because it gives some account of the very early years of his platoon when he was, in his own words, building up 'a crack force of ruthless killers'.

The slip of the pen in the first line is interesting. Mainwaring writes: 'It's now a year since I appointed myself – that is, since I was appointed – commanding officer...'. In fact, in the confusion attending the outbreak of hostilities, it seems that administrative affairs were often a trifle slipshod. My researches reveal that Captain Mainwaring did indeed appoint himself commanding officer of the Walmington-on-Sea Home Guard platoon. But this enterprising, if slightly cheeky, deed caught up with him some years later. We learn from many sources, and notably a letter from Private Frazer to an apparently reclusive brother of his, a retired fisherman in the Hebrides, that the authorities ultimately found out the truth. In part, Frazer's letter reads:

He's for it now. He's been strutting about and lording it over us for years and years and he's no more an officer than one of the codfish you used to catch, Angus. He's just a wee, jumped-up little Sassenach twerp and I wouldnae be surprised if he wasnae court-martialled for impairsonating an officer and shot at dawn. The question is, naturally, who will succeed him. I have to be candid with you, Angus, and say there's not a man jack amongst them that's fit for the job. Whisht, and a puling, doddering, bungling, blathering bunch of incompetent imbeciles they are, and that's putting it mildly. Take the two NCOs. Wilson is mair like some simpering aristocrat at court than a rugged man of action. You can imagine him inhaling a pinch of snuff and tapping his fan on his knee while the court musician plays some dreary dirge of a tuneless air mair than chargin' to meet the foe wie fixed bayonet. Awa' wi' him for a fop and fool! As for the so-called Lance-Corporal – the mon's decrepit. Jones can barely see straight enough to carve a pork chop, which I have to say hasnae appeared amongst the slops and scraps in his shop these several years, never mind to bayonet a Hun. He should be put out to grass in the Butcher's Retreat. For the rest – Walker's a rogue, simply a rogue. If you gave him the platoon, he'd be like as not to sell the Lewis Gun to the enemy. Pike's a puling infant while Godfrey has retreated so far into second childhood it would be a kindness tae tak awa' his rifle and gie him a rattle instead. No, the truth is, Angus, that not one of them is officer material. So I wouldnae be totally surprised, brother, if the next time I write I'll be signing myself 'Captain'. For the rest, business is poor. How are your corns? A good cure is vinegar with a little powdered manure dissolved ....

Perhaps I should correct the impression the above extract may inadvertently convey that Private Frazer was lacking in loyalty to his commanding officer. This was simply not the case. In normal circumstances, and when the platoon was out on exercise and functioning efficiently, there was no more fearless and devoted soldier than this man. But he had a fierce sense of military propriety, allied to a fully justified sense of his own worth, which meant that he kept a beady eye on events and was ever-ready to offer himself for promotion if he thought it would benefit his beloved unit and adopted village.

PRIVATE FRAZER WAS NOT LACKING IN LOYALTY BUT HAD A 'FULLY JUSTIFIED' SENSE OF HIS OWN WORTH.

We know little about his reclusive brother except that he seems to have had bad feet. In the event, Frazer's willingness to assume the leadership of the Walmington platoon was not needed for the platoon rallied to their deposed commander. Many of them wrote letters to the War Office testifying to his excellent leadership, and Mainwaring was, before long, reinstated as CO.

The very first entry in his log, which follows, gives abundant testimony to those bulldog qualities, and that almost intuitive understanding of how to get the best from his troops, which made the Walmington-on-Sea platoon such a splendid fighting unit.

WELL NOW, IT'S a year since I appointed myself – that is, since I was appointed – commanding officer of the Walmington-on-Sea platoon of the Home Guard. In those early days, of course, we were known as Local Defence Volunteers. I was the captain. Wilson was the sergeant and Jones was the lance-corporal. Jones was obviously a bit decrepit. He'd served under General Kitchener or someone like that. In the Sudan or some place. He fought the Fuzzy-Wuzzies – or so he claims. Picked up a lot of tips about the use of the bayonet. Jones's battle-cry is: 'They don't like it up 'em, sir – they don't like it up 'em at all.' Very true.

When Jones signed on he asked if he could have his stripe back. Seems he'd been a lance-corporal when fighting the Mad Mahdi who apparently had a son who was an even Madder Mahdi. According to Jones, that is. Jones was so decrepit he signed the table because he couldn't see the registration slip, and he had a kind of sideways stagger when he turned the corner, so I was doubtful at first if he was NCO material. But Wilson pointed out that we were going to need NCOs and also that Jones was likely to take back the two pounds of steak he'd brought us if we didn't give him his stripe. So we let him have it. And that made up the command structure, you see? Me as captain. Wilson as sergeant and Jones as lance-corporal.

Now I don't like to boast, as everyone who knows me well knows very well indeed, but I have to say that we have pulled it off. We formed our platoon to keep Hitler from invading and he has not, in fact, invaded. Naturally I don't think the entire credit goes to the Walmington-on-Sea platoon. But what I do say is that the existence of keen, tough, fully-trained men, such as we have in our platoon, all round the coasts of the British Isles has been a big factor in keeping him at bay.

Of course he still might invade. Then again at some time in the future, when this show's all over, some other tyrant, not necessarily the Hun, might have another crack at us. And that is the reason why I have decided to keep this log. If another crackpot arises who thinks he can take on England, a log such as the one I propose to keep could be invaluable. Teach future Home

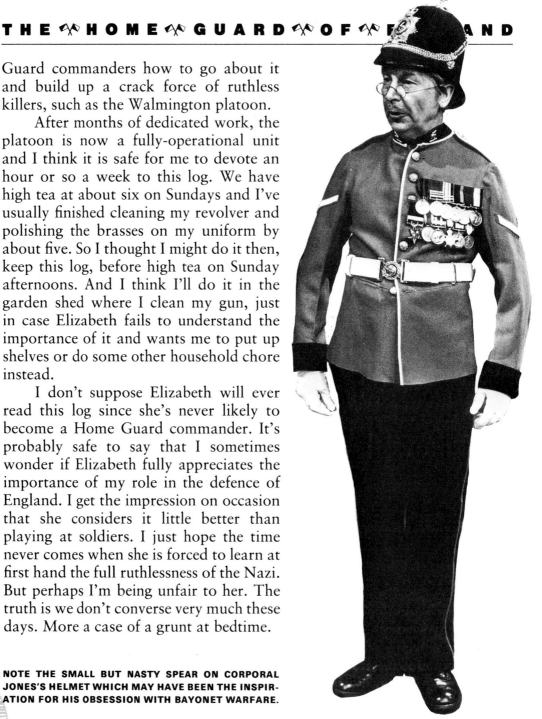

Guard commanders how to go about it and build up a crack force of ruthless killers, such as the Walmington platoon.

After months of dedicated work, the platoon is now a fully-operational unit and I think it is safe for me to devote an hour or so a week to this log. We have high tea at about six on Sundays and I've usually finished cleaning my revolver and polishing the brasses on my uniform by about five. So I thought I might do it then, keep this log, before high tea on Sunday afternoons. And I think I'll do it in the garden shed where I clean my gun, just in case Elizabeth fails to understand the importance of it and wants me to put up shelves or do some other household chore instead.

I don't suppose Elizabeth will ever read this log since she's never likely to become a Home Guard commander. It's probably safe to say that I sometimes wonder if Elizabeth fully appreciates the importance of my role in the defence of England. I get the impression on occasion that she considers it little better than playing at soldiers. I just hope the time never comes when she is forced to learn at first hand the full ruthlessness of the Nazi. But perhaps I'm being unfair to her. The truth is we don't converse very much these days. More a case of a grunt at bedtime.

NOTE THE SMALL BUT NASTY SPEAR ON CORPORAL JONES'S HELMET WHICH MAY HAVE BEEN THE INSPIRATION FOR HIS OBSESSION WITH BAYONET WARFARE.

What I propose to do in this log is give the actual feel of our day-by-day, and week-by-week, operations. Make it feel real and vivid, the way you just never get from training manuals. They don't, for example, tell you what it's like to get sopping wet in a hedgerow all night looking out for enemy parachutists after a reported sighting, only to find in the morning that it was someone's old nightgown blowing in the wind. They don't convey the thrill of stopping an enemy tank dead in its tracks, even if it's not a real tank but Lance-Corporal Jones's butcher's delivery van standing in for one for training purposes. Then there's the comradeship, those precious moments when, after a gruelling forced march or bayonet practice, the command goes out: alright men, let's take a ten-minute break. The command, of course, goes out from me and then the men all relax, perhaps in some convenient haystack, and I get Pike to brew up tea. (No, not Pike, because he's likely to set the stack on fire.) Anyway, we relax with a mug of good old char and perhaps a cigarette and we talk and joke as soldiers do. Someone listening might think we were just rude and licentious soldiery, because Walker's jokes sometimes get a bit

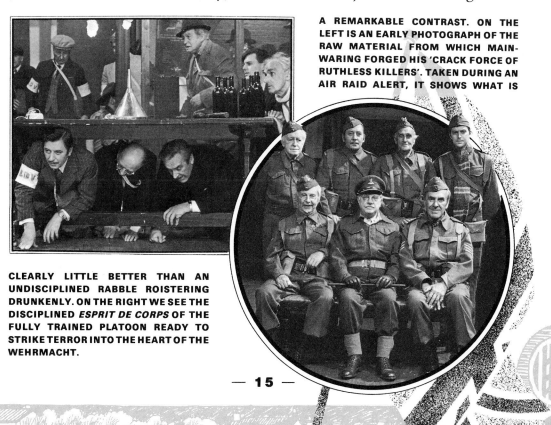

A REMARKABLE CONTRAST. ON THE LEFT IS AN EARLY PHOTOGRAPH OF THE RAW MATERIAL FROM WHICH MAIN-WARING FORGED HIS 'CRACK FORCE OF RUTHLESS KILLERS'. TAKEN DURING AN AIR RAID ALERT, IT SHOWS WHAT IS

CLEARLY LITTLE BETTER THAN AN UNDISCIPLINED RABBLE ROISTERING DRUNKENLY. ON THE RIGHT WE SEE THE DISCIPLINED *ESPRIT DE CORPS* OF THE FULLY TRAINED PLATOON READY TO STRIKE TERROR INTO THE HEART OF THE WEHRMACHT.

EVER ALERT FOR WAYS TO IMPROVE THE MORALE AND CONFIDENCE OF HIS MEN, MAINWARING FREQUENTLY 'DOCTORED' GENUINE PHOTOGRAPHS OF MILITARY OPERATIONS BY SUPERIMPOSING THE FACES OF MEMBERS OF HIS PLATOON ON THEM. HERE WE HAVE A CHARACTERISTIC EXAMPLE OF THE TECHNIQUE. THE OTHER PICTURE SHOWS THE INGENIOUS WAY IN WHICH CORPORAL JONES' ANCIENT (EVEN AT THE TIME!) DELIVERY VAN WAS CONVERTED INTO A DEADLY ASSAULT VEHICLE.

near the knuckle, and never understand how necessary such moments of masculine communion are to the business of soldiering.

Now, what happened last week? Oh, before I come to that I'd better just put you in the picture about our training facilities. We have the use of the Church Hall twice a week for drill and for planning exercises and suchlike. We share the hall with the vicar since, of course, it's his church. But that's no reason why he should get almost hysterical every time he finds a few bits of mud on the floor, is it?

But if the vicar can be a pain in the – well, neck, what about his sourfaced verger? I sometimes think that man gets his salary direct from Berlin. Always snooping and prying about, trying to learn our secrets, and what for? To transmit them back to his masters in Germany? Far-fetched? Possibly, but it's better to be safe than sorry where spies are concerned.

Hodges, the Chief ARP Warden, is another one who does his best to thwart our manoeuvres. For example, if someone lights a match on night patrol to read a map, Hodges springs out of a hedge bawling: 'Put out that light!' Never seems to notice the glare of candles when the vicar's holding a special communion service or when his own wife, Mrs Hodges, takes an oil lamp with her when visiting her outdoor privy. Hodges never seems aware of that. But he does his best to hamper our vital preparations for repulsing the enemy. Actually I would suggest that Hodges is a more likely candidate than the verger for being considered an enemy agent. Alright that may sound a bit strong but I will say this. If Hodges were acting under specific instructions from the Reeks Chancellery, or whatever it's called, to sabotage the Walmington-on-Sea military machine, he could not make a better job of it. I daresay there'll be a full inquiry after the war and I for one won't be posting any files in cakes to Brixton prison if that's where he ends up.

Well now that you're fully in the picture about where and how we train, I'll come to the big event of the week. It all began around closing time – bank closing time, that is – last Tuesday. Oh, before I get into the story proper I ought to tell you that I have recently completed an in-depth study of the strategic problems associated with the defence of Walmington-on-Sea. This study has compelled me to scrap my old battle plan, which is like the following diagram:

You'll see from this diagram that I envisaged a series of strongpoints, each manned by two men and a Lewis gun. The problem is that the platoon only has one Lewis gun and some of the men, such as Corporal Jones and Godfrey, are not quite reliable during long periods of manning remote strongpoints. They have a tendency to fall asleep. The plan also involved a communications problem in that the distance between the strongpoints was too short for carrier pigeons.

I'm an Energy Food!

Says 'POTATO PETE'

DESTROY THIS MAD BRUTE

MILITARISM

KULTUR

ENLIST

U.S. ARMY FOOD MARKETS

Copyright Applied for —

POTATOES
|||||||||||||||||||||||||||||||||||||
GALORE
|||||||||||||||||||||||||||||||||||

If you are fed up with getting tiny potatoes that are like pebbles with a thousand eyes then look no further. At HODGES you will find the spud superb – and as many of them as you want. Also cabbages, onions and carrots. Fruit in season. HODGES is like a pre-war PARADISE for the spud hunter. See for yourself.

IN A LETTER DISCOVERED IN THE DOSSIER, MAINWARING COMPARED HODGES' APPEARANCE TO THAT OF 'THE MAD BRUTE IN THE POSTER'. WAS HE RIGHT?

Jones had some cockeyed scheme for using carrier dogs instead but clearly these would be vulnerable to enemy action. The Hun has never been much of a friend of man's best friend. So with all these considerations in mind I set about totally revising the defences of Walmington-on-Sea and, on the basis of a scientific and logistical study, came up with the following:

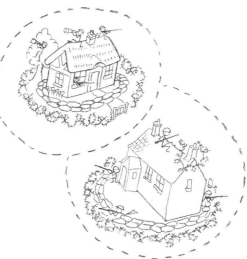

As you will see, it is grounded in the notion of mounting a radial defence focused upon two major redoubts: the Novelty Rock Emporium and Godfrey's Cottage. With suitable sandbagging, which has now been completed, the Novelty Rock Emporium has been converted into a well-nigh impregnable strong point from which to repel invaders coming in from the sea. However, the real key to the defence of Walmington is Godfrey's Cottage which is, from a strategic point of view, superbly placed at a crossroads past which all enemy troops and armour would have to proceed if they were to have a dog's chance of securing their beachhead. It is hardly too much to say that the side which controls Godfrey's Cottage controls the southern defences. Well, possibly that is a bit too much to say, but I would emphasise that its strategic value is immense.

One problem that arose when setting up Godfrey's Cottage as the second bastion of our defences was how to get into the place. It turned out that Godfrey does not have a key. He lives with his two maiden sisters and it seems that they promised him a key years ago but never actually gave him one.

It would be a disaster, obviously, if the invasion began and our Home Guard detachment couldn't get into the cottage. For once, Jones came up with a reasonable solution, which was that Godfrey, and of course his sisters, should always leave the key under a flowerpot on the front porch of the cottage when they were out. In an invasion situation, it would be possible simply to burst down the door, but Godfrey's Cottage is a very pretty affair with rose trellises and suchlike and you might say it was what we're fighting this war to defend. So it would be a pity if our own side had to vandalise it. The flowerpot seemed the best solution.

Alright then, is that clear? This was the situation which pertained last Tuesday evening as I got ready to stop work for the night. Of course it wasn't night really since it was a glorious summer evening and as you know it doesn't get dark these days until very nearly twenty hundred hours, no hang on, that should be eighteen hundred – let's say about ten.

Wilson was with me, checking the day's transactions, when young Pike looked in and said:

'Evening, Mr Mainwaring. Evening, Uncle Arthur. I'll tell mum you'll be in for supper, shall I?'

I couldn't help frowning slightly at hearing this. Of course, I wouldn't dream of prying into the private lives of any of my staff or members of my platoon but Wilson has been with me for many years now and it has sometimes seemed to me that he has something of a rum set-up, and one that could affect discipline especially as regards young Pike.

Wilson, looking a trifle flustered, said: 'Yes, I'll try and make it, Frank.'

'That's good, Uncle Arthur. I like it when we all have supper together. And at bedtime you will go on telling me the story about the princess and the fr – '

'Yes, yes, of course, Frank,' said Wilson hurriedly.

Smiling happily, young Pike departed.

I took the opportunity to say, 'I hope you don't mind my mentioning it, Wilson, but I do think it would be a good idea if young Pike stopped calling you Uncle Arthur. It's bad for discipline in the platoon.'

Wilson sighed and looked abashed. 'I'm sorry, sir,' he apologised. 'It's not really my fault. You see when he was a little boy he used to call me something else, and Mavis – that is to say, Mrs Pike – told him to call me Uncle Arthur in order to – well, stop him calling me – well, the other thing.'

'And what was that?' I asked, determined to get to the bottom of this.

'Daddy,' murmured Wilson, gazing out of the window at some gulls on the public house opposite.

I was taken aback naturally. 'But you and Mrs Pike are not – I mean, she's not – that is, you're not really Pike's daddy – er, father, are you?'

'No, of course not, sir,' Wilson murmured faintly. 'Now I think I'd better go. I promised to collect Frank's sweet ration and the confectioner will close at any moment.'

'What does he have, lollipops?' I asked, not trying too hard to keep the irony out of my voice.

'Only at weekends,' Wilson explained. 'Otherwise it's Fry's chocolate cream bars – when we can get them. Do you mind if I rush, sir?'

Shaking my head wearily, I waved him away. Then I examined my desk, as I do every night, to make sure that nothing confidential would be left on it overnight. In the event I found several documents which belonged in the vaults and I therefore took them down there. Once down in the vaults I recalled that I'd promised Elizabeth that I'd check up on our insurance cover for household property in the event of air-raid damage and I spent twenty minutes or so going through my own safe-deposit box and examining the relevant papers. The upshot was that it was half an hour or so before I got back to my own office. There, to my surprise, I found Corporal Jones in a state of high excitement and Private Frazer looking lugubrious, which is something he does often.

'Don't panic, Captain Mainwaring,'

'DID YE NO HEAR THE BELLS?' THIS IS THE ROLLING-EYED VISION THAT MUST HAVE CONFRONTED MAINWARING WHEN HE CAME UP OUT OF HIS VAULT.

ALL OVER ENGLAND, CHURCH BELLS WERE ON STAND-BY TO PEAL OUT THE DREAD TIDINGS OF INVASION. BUT POSSIBLY ONLY IN WALMINGTON-ON-SEA WERE DEFENCES READY FOR INSTANT ACTIVATION.

cried Jones. 'Don't panic, sir.'

'What are you two doing here?' I asked.

'We've answered the summons,' exclaimed Jones with some fervour. 'We're ready for whatever befalls in this fatal hour, as Mr Churchill said, or am I thinking of General Kitchener who was quite like Mr Churchill in some ways except he didn't smoke cigars and looked different.'

'Be quiet, Jones,' I snapped, realising that something was really amiss.

I turned to the tall Scottish undertaker with the long lean face and the eyes that, as they were doing now, had a strong tendency to roll rather unpleasantly in his head.

'What exactly is going on, Frazer?' I asked.

'Did ye no hear the bells?' he asked portentously.

'What bells?'

'The Chairch bells – pealing the toll of doom. They've come, Captain Mainwaring.'

'Who's come?'

'Well, who do ye think, mon? The Germans.'

'Great Scott,' I exclaimed. 'You mean . . .'

'It would hardly be a wedding at this time of day, would it? The church bells are the signal for invasion.'

I immediately rose to the occasion. 'Right, I'll get my revolver and we'll assemble with the others at the Novelty Rock Emporium.'

'They won't be there, sir,' cried Corporal Jones. 'They've all gone to the pictures in Eastgate.'

'What?' I exclaimed.

'It's true, Captain Mainwaring,' Private Frazer confirmed. 'The outing was arranged some weeks ago. I refused to join them because I resent paying one and sixpence to watch Americans making fools . . .'

'Yes, yes, Frazer,' I silenced him. 'Has the whole platoon gone?'

'All but us and Godfrey.'

'Godfrey doesn't like the Eastgate cinema, sir,' Jones explained. 'Because the gents' toilet is outside in the yard and he . . .'

'Alright, Jones,' I cut him short. 'That leaves Godfrey, us three and Wilson – who should be here now, if he heard the bells. Still, that's not enough to man the Novelty Rock Emporium effectively. So we'll have to fall back on the second line of defence: Godfrey's Cottage.'

'That's right, sir!' exclaimed Jones, jabbing his bayonet eagerly at my desk and causing, as I later discovered, a certain amount of surface damage. 'We'll fight to the last. That's what we'll do, sir, fight to the last. And when

NO LONGER YOUNG, JONES FREQUENTLY SHOWED A TENDENCY TO REEL, TO ROLL, TO LIST OR JUST TO STAGGER ALONG, PANTING HARD.

we run out of ammo we'll give 'em the old cold steel – like this, sir. Oh, sorry about your desk, sir. But they don't like it up 'em, you see, sir. They don't like it . . .'

'Oh, do pull yourself together, Jones,' I urged him.

'Sorry, sir,' he apologised, still dancing about with plunging bayonet. 'It's just that I've got the smell of battle in me nostrils. It gets me going, you know.'

'Aargh!' cried Frazer, as Jones' bayonet sliced open his gas-mask case. 'Put that away, ye daft old fool. Ye're a bigger menace than the Germans.'

'Come on, men,' I ordered. But Frazer hung back.

'It's going to be a wee bit difficult to defend the town with just three men, isn't it, sir?'

'Undoubtedly,' I agreed. 'But the crossroads where Godfrey's Cottage is situated is a key position. Three determined men can hold up an army there. Deny the enemy passage through to London. If we can only hold out long enough, our regular forces will have enough time to re-group for a counter-attack. It might be the end of us of course, but we are prepared for that, aren't we?'

Frazer shook his head slowly. 'Well, it's not the way I'd planned to spend the evening but . . .'

We stepped out of the bank and I flattened myself against the wall.

'What are you doing, Mr Mainwaring?' asked Frazer irritably.

'Do the same,' I ordered. 'I'm surprised at you, Frazer, after all the exercises we've done. There may be snipers out there.'

'Och, dinna be so daft, man,' exclaimed Frazer with what, in other circumstances, I should have been inclined to regard as insubordination. 'The bells are rung when the Germans are spotted setting off across the channel. The first we'll hear of them, in all probability, is their dive-bombers screaming down on us.'

'Then again,' urged Jones, 'they may decide to depend on the element of surprise and paddle quietly ashore in rubber boats and suchlike. Then we'd just see their shadows flitting amongst the trees and we'd have to be ready . . .'

'Oh come along, both of you!' I exclaimed impatiently since I had, by this time, perceived that traffic in the High was pretty much as usual.

At the double, we hastened through the streets of Walmington with our most valuable item of weaponry, the Lewis gun. However, after about a hundred yards of doubling, and aware that Jones and Frazer were no longer men in the prime of life, I gave the order to slow down to normal marching pace. But even this proved taxing to Jones and by the time we approached Godfrey's cottage, on the outskirts of Walmington, he was showing a tendency to stagger along panting hard. I put up my hand for a halt.

'It's alright, sir,' gasped Jones. 'I can . . .'

'Quiet,' I ordered peremptorily.

'What do you hear, sir?' asked Frazer, frowning grimly.

'There,' I exclaimed. 'Don't you hear it? Out to sea? Guns. Eight-inchers, I should imagine.'

We all stood frozen for a few moments and listened. Faint and distant, almost like the sound of a horse-drawn cart, came a far-off rumble.

'I hear it, sir,' cried Jones. 'They're coming! Don't panic! Don't panic!'

Just then, out of a lane ahead of us, rumbled a cart laden with mangel-wurzels and drawn by a sway-backed horse which I recognised as belonging to Rufus Bloggs, a heavily-overdrawn farmer.

'Guns!' sneered Frazer. 'Its only Bloggs off to make some of his moonshine hootch down at the ruined mill. Pity we can't get the Gairmans to sample some of that. They'd be so busy with the trots they wouldna hae time for their invasion any more.'

'That's enough of that, Frazer,' I rebuked the man. 'Come on, one last effort at the double and we'll be at the cottage.'

We could, in fact, see the cottage – a small architectural gem – set in its wonderful, glowing English country garden no more than a quarter of a mile up the road. Less than ten minutes later we were entering through the trim little garden gate and approaching up the front path nicely made out of crazy paving. Since there was a light on – somewhat unpatriotically I felt, since it was still daylight – in the downstairs living room it was clear that someone was at home and there would be no need to use the upturned flowerpot which I perceived beside the door-mat. I raised my hand to knock. I confess I was disagreeably surprised when Frazer knocked my hand away with painful force.

'What the devil!' I exclaimed.

But Frazer, again rather painfully, gripped my arm and in a hoarse whisper said: 'Be silent, sir. It's a trap.'

'What?' I exclaimed, wondering if he'd taken leave of his senses.

'Just be still a moment and listen.'

We all three stood on the porch listening for a short while. Jones put his ear to the door but none of us heard a thing.

'Really, Frazer . . .'

'I haird it, I tell you,' breathed Frazer. 'I wasn't known in the Royal Navy as the human sonar for nothing. I have ears like a lynx – like a lynx. I haird the guttural sound of a German soldier uttering one of the brutal things they do utter.'

'What kind of things, Mr Frazer?' asked Jones eagerly.

'Oh, what does it matter, Jones?' I urged irritably. 'Well, if you're sure, Frazer. Perhaps we'd better do a reconnaissance.'

'Permission to speak, sir?' Jones bawled abruptly, causing Frazer to kick him fiercely on the ankle. Jones thereupon uttered a howl that might have been expected to bring the entire German expeditionary force down on us. But after we had all frozen in apprehension for a moment the danger apparently passed.

'Keep your voice down, Jones,' I instructed the softly moaning corporal.

'Yes, sir. Sorry, sir. I'd just like to volunteer to do the reconnaissance, sir. I could swarm up the rose trellis to the roof and listen down the chimney pots to see what rooms the German are ensconced in, sir, and then I could drop a grenade down the chimney and . . .'

'Shut up, you senile old fool,' suggested Frazer ungraciously. 'All we have to do is listen beneath yon window. We'll be able to tell what's going on.'

'Excellent idea, Frazer,' I complimented him. 'I suppose it's possible that an advance party of skilled saboteurs and Hun commandos has got here ahead of the main force, but it seems on the surface of it unlikely.'

We crept along the side of the house and stationed ourselves under the window. Almost at once we heard voices. But they were not German voices. They were English voices. The first one, which was female, asked:

'Are you enjoying your nice bit of haddock, Charles?'

The second voice replied: 'Yes, thank you.'

That voice was undoubtedly Godfrey's and so we assumed, although none of us had met either of them, that the first voice must have belonged to one of Godfrey's two sisters, Dolly and Cissy.

'Sounds perfectly normal,' I said softly. 'I'm going to take a look.'

'Be careful, sir. Don't get your head up into the line of fire. Keep low, sir. I remember, sir, in the trenches around Harris, as we used to call it, when we was going to . . .'

'Jones!' I cautioned him once more. 'Don't talk any more until I give you permission. Is that understood?'

'Understood, sir. I won't talk any more until I have received permission . . .'

'Jones!'

The excitable corporal at last fell silent. Slowly, I raised my head above the sill of the window and peered through into Godfrey's parlour. I saw him at once, looking like a kind of adult baby, seated at one end of a little dining table, eating haddock. Also at table, drinking tea and eating bread and butter, were two ladies rather older than Godfrey and dressed in a somewhat dated fashion. The younger one, who I have since learned is Dolly, was saying:

THE SCENE MAINWARING, FRAZER AND JONES BEHELD WHEN THEY PEERED THROUGH THE WINDOW. CISSY IS FEEDING THE PARROT WHICH, PURCHASED ORIGINALLY FROM A DRUNKEN SEA-COOK, WAS FAMOUS FOR THE RANGE AND DEPRAVITY OF ITS UTTERANCES. DOLLY AND CISSY WERE TOO DEAF TO HEAR THEM AND GODFREY TOO INNOCENT TO GRASP THEIR MEANING.

'Do you know I had to queue up for twenty minutes this morning just for that little bit of fish.'

The other sister, Cissy, then asked her brother: 'Aren't you parading with the Yeomanry tonight, Charles?'

I lowered my head again. 'Seems perfectly in order,' I informed Jones and Frazer. 'Godfrey's just having his tea with his two sisters. I wonder where she gets that haddock? I haven't seen any for months.'

'I haird a German voice,' insisted Frazer stubbornly.

'I have it, sir,' exclaimed Jones, disobeying my order to keep quiet. 'The Germans are probably in there hiding behind the door in the cupboard and they have their guns trained on Godfrey and his sisters telling them to act natural or they'll blow them to kingdom come.'

'Why would they be doing that, Jones?' I asked sceptically.

A SPLENDID EXAMPLE OF MAIN-WARING'S TRAINING TECHNIQUE OF SUPERIMPOSING THE FACES OF PLATOON MEMBERS ON PHOTO-GRAPHS OF ACTUAL OPERATIONS. (NOTE: IT IS NOT RECORDED THAT THE WALMINGTON-ON-SEA PLATOON EVER ENGAGED IN AIR-BORNE ACTIVITIES.)

'I don't know, sir,' confessed the corporal. 'Well perhaps they've found out we're coming to take over this strongpoint and they've laid a trap for us or –'

'I'm going to have a look,' said Frazer firmly.

We all three very cautiously raised our head above the sill until we could see the three old people at their high tea. All seemed perfectly normal. As we watched, Godfrey got to his feet.

'Do you really have to go again, dear?' asked Cissy sadly. 'You went just before tea.'

'No, no, I just wanted to try the wireless again,' Godfrey reassured her. 'When that rather unpleasant war play is over I'd like to listen to the Palm Court Orchestra.'

Godfrey crossed over to where the wireless set stood on a small, dark oak table. He switched it on and stood waiting for it to warm up. In a little while a voice came from it.

'You may haff captured me, Colonel Smith, but I vill tell you nothing. As a soldier of the Führer I am glad to die for the fatherland and I have only one thing to say to a decadent democrat like you –'

'It's still going on,' said Dolly with a sigh. 'I do wish the war would end. It's having such a bad effect on radio drama.'

Godfrey switched off the set again and returned to the table. I looked at Frazer quizzically but he shrugged dismissively.

'You have to admit, it was a Gairman voice, Captain Mainwaring.'

We thereupon returned to the front door and knocked. There was a pause and then Godfrey's friendly, if faintly imbecilic, face presented itself to us. He looked astonished. 'Captain Mainwaring!' he exclaimed. 'What are you doing here?'

I ignored this asinine question.

'Didn't you hear the bells?' I snapped.

Godfrey smiled with that vacant, babyish smile which sometimes makes me wonder if he is really quite as ruthless as I expect my platoon to be.

'Bells?' he asked, wonderingly. 'No, I didn't. What kind of bells?'

'The church bells.'

'Oh, how delightful, sir,' he enthused. 'I'm so sorry we missed them.' He glanced over his shoulder and then leaned forwards confidentially. 'I fear Dolly and Cissy are just a little hard of hearing. Still, now that you're here why don't you, Corporal Jones and Private Frazer join us for tea?'

I sighed. 'Godfrey, get your rifle and steel helmet. The invasion's begun.'

Godfrey frowned at this intelligence. 'Oh dear,' he said disapprovingly. 'I thought it might happen sooner or later but I had hoped I'd be able to get the roses pruned before – '

'Godfrey,' I snapped, 'don't you understand that at this very moment the Hun is probably storming ashore on the marine parade? I want to set up a machine-gun nest here to keep them penned in the coastal salient.'

'That's a bit awkward, sir,' said Godfrey unhappily.

'Oh? Why?'

'Well, I'm not at all sure how Dolly and 'Cissy will take it. You see they take such beautiful care of the cottage, always polishing and –'

'You mean you didn't tell them? That this cottage is now a designated strongpoint?'

'I'm afraid not, sir. I tried to several times but I felt it would upset them. And so – '

I shook my head incredulously. 'Well, I'm very sorry, Godfrey, but I'm afraid the defence of the realm takes precedence over your furniture.'

I turned to Jones and Frazer. 'Come on. Let's find the window with the best line of fire for the Lewis gun.'

Thus began a period of feverish activity.

Jones's eyesight is not quite up to sniper's standards and so it was Frazer and I who examined the field of fire commanded by each of the windows. We settled on the south-west window covering the garden with its revolving summer-house and beyond that the Western Approaches to Walmington-on-Sea. As we were setting up the Lewis gun there, Godfrey hurried up to us with a rather attractive knitted doily.

'Would you mind putting the

VERA LYNN, THE SWEETHEART OF THE FORCES.

gun on this, Captain Mainwaring? I'm so afraid of that regency desk getting scratched.'

I sighed but permitted poor old Godfrey to retain the illusion that life would go on much the same after this fateful day. I simply couldn't bring myself to explain that doilies and horse brasses were unlikely to survive the fury that was coming. I must say Cissy and Dolly behaved with exemplary aplomb. Indeed, as I watched them sitting placidly knitting and listening to Vera Lynn, the sweetheart of the forces, I could not help feeling that, if they had been fit young men rather than old ladies, they would have been an ornament to the platoon.

We needed sandbags for the gun emplacement and to reinforce the other windows and, of course, had none. So Frazer and Jones went round the house collecting every cushion they could find and then filling the covers with coal from the capacious coal cellar. It was clear that this part of our warlike preparations distressed Godfrey inordinately and so I made him go up to the guest room and keep watch for Germans so that he wouldn't witness the desecration. I only let him down again when the coal-bagging was complete and the cottage had been turned into a fortress.

He returned to the parlour to find Cissy at last beginning to notice the strange activities in her living room.

'Charles, I don't quite understand why Captain Mainwaring and his friends are blocking up our windows?'

'It can't be helped, Cissy,' explained Godfrey loudly. 'You see, the Germans are coming.'

'Oh dear,' she exclaimed. 'I really don't think we can manage any more for tea.'

But she then resumed her knitting and even when the bullets began to fly showed no sign of alarm. And nor did Dolly. I suspect that Godfrey's two sisters were far deafer than he had let on.

I suddenly noticed something and barked: 'Corporal Jones, where's your helmet?'

Jones reached up and felt the top of his pate which was quite bare and unprotected. 'Oh blimey, sir,' he admitted, 'in all this confusion I'm afraid I forgot it.'

'But you must have a steel helmet – or you'll fall victim to the first stray bullet,' I insisted.

'A LITTLE LIKE HINDENBURG ON A BAD DAY'? CORPORAL JONES READY FOR THE BATTLE OF GODFREY'S COTTAGE.

At this point a happy thought clearly struck Godfrey for he smiled like a baby in an Ovaltine advertisement. Then he went to one of the windows, opened it, reached out, fiddled about for a moment and brought into the parlour a kind of pot with geraniums growing in it.

'You can use this, Corporal Jones,' he enthused, handing it to the puzzled soldier.

I shook my head irritably. 'Godfrey, if you'd read the firearms manual more carefully you'd have realised that earthenware will not stop a high-velocity rifle bullet.'

'Oh no, Captain Mainwaring – it's a steel helmet – a German one. I brought it back from France in 1918 as a souvenir.'

He thereupon held it out of the window and emptied the earth out of it and sure enough a perfectly serviceable steel helmet was revealed in the characteristic shape still used by the German Army today.

'Well,' I said approvingly. 'That's different. Put it on, Jones.'

Jones did so and, apart from making him look a little like Hindenburg on a bad day, it fitted very well.

And now, with our preparations complete there was nothing for it but to wait.

We had only waited about ten minutes when Jones suddenly exclaimed 'Ooh er!' and did a strange wriggle as if practising to be a belly dancer or something of that sort.

'What is it, Jones?' I asked coldly. I suspected he was playing the fool to keep our spirits up and while I admired his courage I didn't want any distraction from the grim business of keeping watch for the enemy.

'I've got a cold wriggly feeling down my spine, sir,' he explained.

The man was in the grip of blue funk.

'Oh pull yourself together, Jones,' I said scornfully. 'You've been in action before.'

'Yes,' he conceded, 'but I've never had a cold wriggly feeling down my spine like this before. Ooh er ow oh – there it goes again.'

He squirmed about like one of those dancing girls in that soldiers' place in France that we used to – that I heard about. Then he put his hand inside his shirt at the back, groped about for a moment and brought out a long dangling earthworm. I was relieved to find my suspicions had been wrong.

'What shall I do with this, sir?' he asked.

'It wouldnae make a cheerful pet,' proclaimed Frazer, who is, of course, an undertaker.

'Kill it, Jones,' I told him.

'Oh, I couldn't do that, sir,' he exclaimed in a shocked tone of voice.

'But you're a butcher, aren't you?'

NATURALLY, WITH A CORPS COMPOSED SUBSTANTIALLY OF VETERANS, RHEUMATISM WAS A SERIOUS MILITARY HAZARD. ABOVE WE SEE AN INGENIOUS TECHNIQUE FOR DEALING WITH A RHEUMATIC EMERGENCY IN THE FIELD.

HOME GUARDS—

Beware of Hitler's unseen ally!—rheumatism

LAST winter you spent your nights in your own warm bed. Now you spend your nights in coldness, wind and rain. Watch out for rheumatism!

It is easy to make light of the first assaults of this old foe of the human race. What are a few aches and twinges to a man who is serving his country? But once rheumatism gets a grip on you, it will take months, or even years, to drive it out

of suffering and incapacity. If you have already allowed rheumatism to get a strong grip on your system, then go to your doctor at once. Almost certainly you will find that he will prescribe Kruschen as part of your treatment. But if rheumatism is just making its first attacks on you—take Double Action Kruschen. Take a teaspoonful in hot water, first thing every

'Very true, sir. But I never get to know the chops and steaks while they're still alive, if you see what I mean, sir. I've been on close terms with this worm. Permission to take it out into the garden and put it on a rose bed, sir?'

I sighed and took a long searching glance about the garden. It was madness, of course, but we had to get rid of the worm somehow and I had an idea it would upset Dolly and Cissy to come upon it indoors.

'Oh, alright, Jones,' I agreed. 'But out and back in like lightning now.'

'Naturally, sir,' agreed the corporal, whereupon he lumbered over to the door, dangling the worm in front of him, and opened it. He tripped over the doormat, lurched down the garden, skidded sideways, dropped the worm on the garden path and gave a loud shout as, accompanied by a bang, a bullet whistled past his head.

'My God, sir,' exclaimed Frazer. 'They're there after all. Perhaps they have been all along. Well that's the end of Corporal Jones. He'll never make it back to our lines.'

'Jones,' I bawled. 'Get back here, man. They're firing at you.'

Jones needed no prompting. He turned, lurched to one side, fell into a rosebush, picked himself up, trundled away in the wrong direction, noticed his error, turned, trotted back towards us and, with a perfect fusillade of shots whistling round him the whole time, tottered through the front door and collapsed gasping into a chair. I slammed the door shut behind him and bolted it.

'You've got a charmed life,' pronounced Frazer, bending over Jones and inspecting him for wounds. 'It must have been all that tumbling about like a clown that confused them.'

'Did you see where their shots were coming from, Frazer?' I asked the gaunt Scot.

'Aye, I did, sir. From the summer house,' he replied.

'Right,' I said. 'We'll soon flush them out. Man the Lewis gun.'

In a disciplined way, Jones and Frazer manned the gun, Frazer at the trigger and Jones feeding magazines.

'Have you got the range, Frazer?' I asked.

'I have, sir.'

'Then – fire!'

At once a deafening tattoo filled the interior of Godfrey's little cottage, so loud that even Cissy and Dolly looked up from their knitting and frowned disapprovingly. With the very first shots, the summer-house, which must have been very delicately balanced, started turning slowly. By the time Jones had inserted the second magazine it was turning quite merrily. When the fourth magazine was reached the little building was spinning like a Catherine wheel. It was then that the enemy, rendered giddy by the implacable fusillade, came reeling from the summer house one by one and, dropping their rifles, staggered about the lawn.

'We've got them!' I enthused, drawing my pistol. 'It's quite obvious that they're incapable of offensive action. I'm going out to take them prisoner.'

'I'll accompany you, sir,' proclaimed Jones loyally. 'With my fixed bayonet.'

He seized his rifle and bayonet. I opened the front door and together we charged out into the garden of Godfrey's cottage to take our first prisoners.

'Hands up! That is: handen hocken!' I said grimly to a tall German who was still reeling about on the lawn.

The German said: 'Good heavens, sir. Is that you?'

'Sergeant Wilson!' I gasped.

The other two Germans turned out to be Pike and Walker. We later learned that Wilson and Pike had, at the first peal of the church bells, hurried down to the Novelty Rock Emporium according to the basic plan for the defence of Wal-mington that I had worked out. Walker, who should have been with the cinema party at East-gate, had, in fact, stayed behind to inspect a consignment of ex-service boots that he was inter-ested in acquiring. He too had made his way to the Novelty Rock Emporium. When no one

CONCEIVABLY THE MOST SENSATIONAL ITEM IN THE WHOLE MAINWARING DOSSIER. PERHAPS IT WAS NOT, AFTER ALL, 'MISCHIEVOUS SCHOOLBOYS' WHO RANG THE INVASION ALERT....

else had turned up there Wilson, as senior rank present, had decided to retreat in an orderly fashion to Godfrey's Cottage. But they had no sooner installed themselves in the summer-house than they observed Jones taking the worm out into the garden. Jones, of course, was wearing a German army helmet and so Wilson and his men naturally assumed the cottage was in enemy hands.

So there you are. The church bells, we found out later, had been rung by two mischievous schoolboys who had managed to get into the bell tower. But I, for one, did not deplore their mischief too much. It gave me a chance to observe the conduct of my men under actual battle conditions. And I think any reader will agree that no field commander could have had greater reason for satisfaction than me. Naturally I was a little disappointed that Wilson's detachment had not managed to hang on inside the revolving summer-house in order to return our withering fire but Pike explained that it was worse than being on a fairground 'whiplash', whatever that is, and they had all been hurled out of the summer-house by centrifugal force.

It was just as well, perhaps, or one detachment or the other might have suffered a casualty, and now that I know the mettle of my men I would be sorry to lose a single one of them. Alright, it was only a rehearsal for the real thing, but none of the actors knew that. We all thought the balloon had gone up and I think we acquitted ourselves satisfactorily. Possibly the only negative aspect of the whole episode was the fact that we had to contribute £4 17s. 3d. from platoon funds to compensate Godfrey for the damage to his cushions, his summer-house and for some mysterious scratches on his dining table that Cissy found and swore had not been there before our arrival. Odd that, because we never touched the dining table. The Lewis gun was set up on the regency desk and that was perfectly adequately protected by Dolly's knitted doily. It suffered no damage at all.

WE ARE FORTUNATE in having a view of these events from a totally different perspective. It seems that Godfrey had a third sister, called Maidie, who, at fifty-one, was the youngest of the family. She had emigrated to America before the war and married a dentist. The Mainwaring Dossier includes a number of letters from the three siblings in Godfrey's cottage to Maidie and a number of Maidie's letters to them. One of the letters from

Cissy to Maidie deals with the very events described in Mainwaring's own log concerning the battle of the cottage.

We lead, as always, very quiet lives here in our little rural retreat. Indeed the only social activity we have experienced in recent months was when some yeomen belonging to the regiment with which Charles regularly marches and drills called unexpectedly. They seem to have looked in on impulse while out on regimental business in the countryside since they brought with them a rather large gun. Naturally we invited them to tea which they accepted although Dolly was a little disappointed that they showed no interest whatsoever in her excellent upside-down cakes. They were led by a man called Mainwaring who apparently found ordinary daylight an affliction. He insisted on filling a lot of our best cushion covers with coal and blocking up the windows with them. In other ways he was a perfectly civil man but kept looking at his watch and muttering about some other guests – Germans, I think he said – whom he was expecting and who, in the event, never showed up at all. The men with him, of lower rank, proved rather rough diamonds and concluded their visit by firing their gun very noisily out of the window. We have asked Charles not to encourage his yeomen friends to drop in unexpectedly again. As regards the war, I can honestly say, Maidie, that we hardly notice it. Life goes on much as ...

A letter from my uncle to my father also concerns itself with the Godfrey's Cottage incident, naturally from the point of view of, from Mainwaring's perspective, 'the enemy'.

...Spot of excitement round here last week, Barney, caused by two village brats getting into the church and ringing the bells. Yes, you can guess the result. Since bell-ringing at any time is the agreed signal for invasion by the barbarian hordes across the channel, half the platoon, including our gallant CO, jumped to the conclusion the big show had started. I was sceptical myself but I thought, for form's sake, I should go through the motions and I went down to the seafront where Mainwaring has set up an HQ in – God help us – an old sweet factory that used to make and sell (by the ton I believe) that ghastly sickly rock stuff. Well, there was no one there and so I took my chaps – Frank and a spiv called Walker (to put the entire Wehrmacht to flight) – on to the other strongpoint, the cottage of a decent old dodderer called Godfrey. Very pretty affair with

rose trellises and suchlike. Just in case Jerry should be in occupation we ensconced ourselves in a revolving summer-house in the grounds and before long – on my oath, Barney – a Hun soldier staggered out of the cottage. Well, we loosed a few rounds on him and the blighter reeled about the garden (drunk we assumed) before retiring unscathed back into the cottage. Then all hell broke loose. The presumptive Huns inside the cottage let loose on our summer-house with a machine-gun which had the effect of causing it to spin round like a fairground roundabout. Three or four minutes of this was enough to send us all reeling dizzily out into the garden careless of whether or not we'd be shot. I dimly perceived a German officer march out of the cottage and demand in bad German: 'Handen hocken' or whatever the Kraut say when they want you to put your hands up. The 'Kraut's' German was so bad that I peered more closely and saw it was really little Mainwaring brandishing his six-shooter. The whole thing had been the most enormous cock-up, Barney. The German soldier we thought we'd seen proved to have been L/Cpl Jones wearing a First World War souvenir for some reason. In other words it had been a small-scale civil war. Little Mainwaring went about crowing over it for days. Thinks it proves what a lot of heroes he's got in his platoon. I think it shows we're all a bunch of under-trained dolts who might easily have shot each other's arses off. Heigh ho. What a way to spend a lifetime. Incidentally, Barney, that bottle of '32 claret that you very kindly sent me was quite superb. Can't tell you how much your letters and the occasional princely gift of that kind mean to me in this backwater . . .

(Extract from letter from Arthur Wilson to Sir Barnington Wilson of Danbigh, Yorks, 1941.)

THE NEXT ENTRY that I have selected for print from Captain Main-waring's tremendous log is an amusing, even in parts hilarious, episode in this Home Guard commander's life. His platoon sergeant goes through a spell of most erratic behaviour for which Mainwaring can find no explanation. Even more risible is the matter of the pigeons which begin to haunt his HQ. But I do not want to spoil your pleasure in discovering for yourselves the intricacies of this period in Mainwaring's military history.

♦ ❬ ❬ ◆ ❭ ❭ ♦

EXTRAORDINARY SEQUENCE OF events last week which shows up the special difficulties of being a Home Guard commander. Could never have happened in the regular army – whatever it was that *did* happen. I think I know how the church got full of feathers, but why Sergeant Wilson acted as he did is more than I can fathom.

First thing I heard about it was when I was taking a special drill parade in the church hall. The fact is: I shouldn't have been taking it at all. Beneath the dignity of a commissioned officer to drill his men, except on special ceremonial occasions such as when the sovereign comes to visit. Thus far the sovereign has not made a visit to Walmington-on-Sea and so it's not been incumbent on me to take a drill parade.

Naturally Sergeant Wilson should have been taking the parade. Quite frankly, I always have some misgivings about Wilson's prowess as a drill-master. RSMs in the Coldstream Guards do not, like Wilson, suggest pleasantly: 'Now then, shall we all come to attention?' Not a bit of it. They thunder out the command, putting the fear of God into their men, who snap into the drill movement like well-oiled machines. Of course, you could say that the whole platoon could do with a bit more oiling – especially Corporal Jones, who has a tendency to spin round on the spot. But we allow Jones a good deal of latitude because he is decidedly a veteran, unlike many of the platoon who are young and keen as mustard. Because of Corporal Jones's

Dear Mr. Mainwaring,

Frank's caught another cold. I have asked you many times to make sure he wears a scarf and ear muffs when he's on duty these cold nights. But Frank says when he tries to put them on you make him take them off. I won't have this, Mr Mainwaring. Frank's health comes first. So if you want him to go on being in your platoon you'll have to look after him better. I suggest next time he's out on one of these bitter nights he has a hot water bottle under his battle-dress. I shall expect you to make sure that he does. And I'll tell Arthur to watch you to see that you do it. And while I'm at it, it seems a long time since I had a statement showing interest on my credit account.

Yours sincerely
Mrs Mavis Pike

very individual style of drill I could hardly ask him to take the parade in Sergeant Wilson's absence. And that was the question which was buzzing about the platoon. Where was Sergeant Wilson?

He had not been seen for days. Not like Wilson to go AWOL. So I was sitting in my office, preparatory to taking the parade, when there was a knock at the door. I barked the order: 'Come in.' And young Pike, who cuts quite a presentable figure except for a slight tendency to pout like an infant, entered smartly.

'Ah, Pike,' I greeted him. 'Any news about Sergeant Wilson?'

'He's not at mum's, Captain Mainwaring.'

I shook my head sadly and commented: 'It's most unlike Wilson. What one has always said about him is that he's dependable. If he's not appeared by this evening, I shall have to contact the police.'

When I said this I observed Pike closely since I had made the pronouncement more to draw him out than because I really felt it was a police matter. Wilson has a rather special relationship with young Pike, and possibly Mrs Pike as well, and I felt that any mention of the police would bring about a reaction. I was not disappointed. An anxious look immediately sprang into Pike's eyes, and he stammered:

'I wouldn't do that if I were you, Mr. Mainwaring.'

I nodded sagely and, to encourage further confidences, contented myself with saying 'Oh?' on a rising inflection. Again this produced results.

'I expect he'll turn up sooner or later,' insisted Pike.

I smiled confidentially and leaned across my desk towards the bewildered young man.

'Are you hiding something?' I asked crisply. And then, before he had a chance to collect his wits, and with something of the benign intonation of a Dutch uncle, or an English one come to that, I urged: 'Come on – out with it, boy.'

What I'm trying to get at is the golden rule for the Home Guard commander: know your men. That's the key to building a successful military force. The regular army may have bigger tanks. Well, actually we haven't got any tanks at all. The army may have all the logistical support, but when it comes to the human relationship, which is all-important, the Home Guard comes into its own. I pride myself that I know every detail, so long as it's relevant to military matters of course, about my men. No uncle in Holland was ever so intimately informed about the state of his men as I am. And now I knew that Pike would tell me what I needed to know.

'Well,' stammered Pike. 'The night before last, he and mum had words.'

I nodded in satisfaction. 'Now we're getting somewhere. What about?'

'Well, I was in bed at the time,' confessed Pike. 'I couldn't hear much leaning over the banisters. But he shouted at mum and she threw him out the front door and threw his ration book after him.'

'Go on,' I urged in a kindly but firm tone of voice.

'Well, after he'd thrown pebbles at her window, she shouted: "Clear off, you beast!" And then she chucked something at him and it broke.'

I nodded grimly. 'I'm beginning to understand.'

Full of trust now, Pike hastened on: 'Well, she got up in the morning and picked up the pieces – all but the handle.'

'Yes, yes, I understand,' I said hastily. 'Alright, Pike, you can go.'

After he'd left my office, I sat and brooded as to what all this meant. I was not totally surprised by Pike's information. I had several times, passing a group of my men when they had not realised I was near, heard strange rumours about Wilson. For example, I heard Walker say: 'Cor, that young girl Wilson was with wasn't half smashing!' On another occasion, I heard Frazer, in his rolling Scottish accent, opine: 'The auld fool's got himself a young gairl – it'll be the ruin of him – just you see – the ruin!' Putting this information together with what Pike had just told me, I began to feel that the key to Wilson's mysterious absence must lurk in the well-known French expression: *churchay la fam*, meaning 'there's a woman mixed up in all this somewhere'.

I nodded in satisfaction at having unravelled this much of the mystery and strode out of my office into the church hall where the men were drawn up ready for drill practice. As always my heart swelled with pride at the thought that this splendid body of English soldiery constituted the platoon that I had founded and formed from scratch. I had no doubts that these men would follow me onto the field of battle should it ever become necessary.

'Right, men,' I addressed them sternly, so they would never guess at the lump in my throat, and then my voice acquired a military ring and, like the born leader I am, I gave the word of command: 'Stand at ease.' I waited a moment or two for Jones to stop revolving before giving my men a bit of a pep talk, as the Yanks call it. I began with an announcement: 'On Sunday,

A SAD DECLINE? WILSON'S OWN SKETCH, FROM A LETTER TO HIS BROTHER, OF HIS CONDITION WHEN DISCOVERED IN AN INTOXICATED STATE BY MAIN-WARING IN THE CHURCH HALL. SUPERIMPOSED ARE STUDIES OF TWO OF HIS (AND MY) RELATIVES SHOWING THE INTERNATIONAL PINNACLES SCALED BY THE FAR-FLUNG WILSON CLAN. NOTE ALSO THE REMARKABLE FAMILY RESEMBLANCE THAT HAS PERSISTED DOWN THE AGES. ABOVE IS AN OIL PAINTING OF MARÉCHAL OUILSON WHO WAS ONE OF NAPOLEON'S MOST TRUSTED COM-MANDERS AND LEFT A PHOTOGRAPH OF GRAF UNTERFÜHRER VON WILSON WHO WAS, ALAS, EXECUTED AFTER HAVING BOLDLY JOINED THE PLOT TO ASSASSINATE HITLER.

HOLDING THE LINE!

A GOOD-HUMOURED BORROWING OF MAINWARING'S OWN TECHNIQUE OF SUPERIMPOSING FACES ON PUBLISHED MATERIAL. AS A TRIBUTE TO HIS LION-HEARTED COMMANDER, AN UNKNOWN MEMBER OF THE PLATOON HAS DOCTORED THIS WARTIME POSTER WHICH ORIGINALLY SHOWED WINSTON CHURCHILL IN THE GUISE OF A BULLDOG.

there will be a voluntary church parade – and I shall expect you all to attend.'
Then I came to the heart of the matter. 'Now, your arms drill is getting very
sloppy. You may not think this is very important but I prefer to go into battle
with tidy soldiers rather than with sloppy and shoddy soldiers. So we're going
to brass it up. Now as Sergeant Wilson isn't with us tonight, I shall take the
drill myself. Right, properly at ease, everyone. Squad – '

At this point there was the most extraordinary interruption. From somewhere at the rear of the ranks came a sound that can hardly be described as
anything but a long groan: aaarghooooer – like that, only more dismal, if you
understand me. I contented myself with a sharp look and the order: 'Silence
in the ranks'.

Then I tried again to start the parade: 'Squad – ' and again the fearful
moan was heard. This time I perceived that it had come not from the ranks
of my men but from behind the curtain on the rostrum. Alert to the possibility
of foul play I promptly drew my revolver, strode over to the curtain and
pulled it back. A most unexpected sight met my eyes. Wild-eyed, dishevelled
and brandishing a bottle that had clearly contained powerful spirit was
Sergeant Wilson. I gaped at him for a moment. And then exclaimed fiercely:

'Wilson!'

He blinked up at me blearily from the pile of old furniture on which he
was sprawled and said in strangled tones:

'Terribly sorry, sir, I didn't realise it was you. I think I must have dropped
off.'

'Go to my office at once,' I ordered him.

A few moments later, having passed in front of the ranks of openly
sniggering men, Wilson and I confronted each other in my office.

'Now, Wilson,' I said severely, 'what's the meaning of this?'

He blinked at me again and swayed on his feet.

'Terribly sorry, sir,' he apologised. 'I feel a bit dizzy. I think I'd better
sit down.' Then, when he had done so, he murmured, 'You must think all
this is very strange.'

'Wilson,' I asked narrowly. 'Have you been drinking?'

'Oh yes, sir,' he conceded at once. 'I've certainly been doing that. I've
been drinking alright. You see, sir – well, actually it all began many years
ago – just after – that is two years after – after the last – '

I noticed that Wilson kept glancing over my right shoulder as if at some alarming presence.

'What is it?' I snapped.

'I'm sorry, sir,' he apologised. 'I keep seeing birds.'

'Pull yourself together, man,' I ordered. 'If you want my advice you'll sign the pledge. You keep going off into a dream. I'm not going to sit here and listen to your meanderings. There's a war on. Those troops have got to be trained. If you want to remain part of this platoon, you'll get out there and give them half an hour's arms drill.'

I must say I was impressed with Wilson's response. The man was clearly a candidate for a hospital bed rather than a parade ground, but he pulled himself to his feet and, with a very game smile on his pale countenance, said: 'Of course, sir.'

Then, reeling visibly, he left my office, closing the door behind him. But the aggravations of the evening were far from over. I devoted myself to paperwork for a time, listening, with that sixth sense the good commander develops, to the hoarse barks of Wilson taking weapons drill outside in the Church Hall. Before long, however, Wilson was back in my office in order to complain that Private Pike was refusing to obey his orders. Realising that this was a very serious offence, even punishable by firing squad, I immediately summoned Pike and demanded an explanation. I was astonished by what he said.

'Mum said that I'm to ignore Sergeant Wilson.'

Naturally I gaped at him in amazement. It's not something I like doing, since it has a tendency to compromoise the dignity appropriate to command, but I had never heard such an outrageous statement in my life.

'Am I hearing you right?' I finally asked.

Pike was not in the least fazed by my grim demeanour. 'Yes, Mr Mainwaring,' he came back quite cheerfully. 'She said if I were to see Unc- Sergeant Wilson I was to ignore him. So I did.'

It is at times like these that the wisdom of the great Home Guard commander is put on trial. Naturally it would have been easy to threaten Pike with dire penalties but what would it have done for the morale of my platoon? Punched a hole in it, that's what. The most important thing a Home Guard unit can have is esprit de corpse, so I couldn't simply have Pike dragged off in irons, could I? I had to be a Dutch uncle once more.

'Now look here, you stupid boy,' I began.

BECAUSE HIS MYSTERIOUS PROFESSION OF OBTAINING ESSENTIAL SUPPLIES NECESSITATED FRE-QUENT VISITS TO THE CAPITAL, WALKER HAD A WAY OF TURNING UP LATE ON PARADE AND STILL IN WHAT MIGHT CHARITABLY BE CALLED 'CIVILIAN DRESS'. SUCH IRREGULARITIES WERE TOLERATED BY MAINWARING IN THE INTERESTS OF KEEPING THE PLATOON FULLY MANNED AND ALSO, PERHAPS, OF OBTAINING THE OCCASIONAL 'UNDER THE COUNTER' BOTTLE OF PRECIOUS SCOTCH.

And then I stopped because I noticed with surprise that Pike was gazing over my right shoulder just as Sergeant Wilson had been doing a little while before.

'What are you looking at, Pike?' I asked irritably.

'Those pigeons, Captain Mainwaring,' he returned in a tone of wonder. 'Why have you got them all over your office?'

At this I naturally turned and, to my distress and surprise, found that the whole place was indeed hopping with pigeons. Behind me a row of pigeons was desecrating the vicar's books. Through the front door darted the verger with a pigeon perched on his head. From the way he was wailing it might have been a German parachutist. A moment later Corporal Jones and Private Walker rushed in and set about trying to catch the pigeons. I gathered that the birds were the result of some kind of transaction between them, but my enquiries were halted by the wretched creatures fluttering in my face. I found this intensely disagreeable and, still wiping my eyes with my handkerchief, left the office, summoning Private Walker to accompany me.

'Have you got anything to do with this, Walker?' I demanded.

The man was clearly flustered and incapable of giving other than ridiculous excuses.

'Well – er – yes, sir. You see, I had this friend who was a pigeon fancier. Only he don't fancy them no more. So I thought you might be able to train them to take messages.'

'Where are they coming from?' I asked sternly.

'From the boiler house next door.'

'And what do you – '

But at this point the door to my office was opened by some idiot and a cloud of pigeons came surging out, followed by half the platoon trying to catch them. There was no more opportunity for speech.

I next encountered the pigeons, or some of them, when we were on night duty in the bunker to the west of Walmington. There was a raid on and the silver bombers droning overhead were sometimes picked out by searchlights or the golden bursts of ack-ack shells.

'It's a fine barrage they're putting up tonight,' Frazer remarked.

Frazer may be a prophet of doom and gloom, which is no asset to the Home Guard commander, but his courage is unquestioned. I think it is fair to say that I have never seen Private Frazer, even in the most hazardous situation, display the slightest hint of funk.

'Yes,' I agreed. 'Three point sevens mostly, I should think.' Then I turned to Private Pike who was crouched next to me with his fingers in his ears. 'Put on the – Pike! Take your fingers out of your ears! You're not a baby any more. You're a member of a front-line fighting platoon.'

'Yes, Mr Mainwaring,' he agreed. 'I just never could stand loud noises. My mum'll tell you that. Once when I was at junior school – '

'Yes, yes, we haven't time for all that now. I was going to say: put the wireless on. We're missing the nine o'clock news.'

Pike went to get his home-made but, considering what a stupid boy he is, quite efficient wireless set and at that moment Walker came up to me and handed me two objects.

'These are for you, Captain Mainwaring – to make up for the other night. I never thought those pigeons would wake up when they did.'

I looked at the objects he had handed me. They were two dressed pigeons.

Should the very worst happen –

as in wartime it often does – there is comfort in knowing that in

FRAZER'S

UNDERTAKING PARLOUR

you still get pre-war standards of service. Funerals to suit every pocket. Let us handle all the details and, like your loved ones, you will find peace.

Service with a mournful smile.

WRITE FOR TASTEFUL,

BLACK-BORDERED

BROCHURE. BOX NO. 193.

STAFF SHORTAGES SPARED NO ONE. PRIVATE FRAZER, WALMINGTON'S UNDERTAKER, PERSONALLY BURIES A DIMINUTIVE CLIENT.

AN ASTONISHING ITEM. THIS PHOTOGRAPH APPEARS TO SHOW PRIVATE WALKER IN THE ACTUAL ACT OF PURLOINING PIGEONS FROM THE 'HEART OF EMPIRE'. HOWEVER, PHOTOGRAPHIC EXPERTS TO WHOM I HAVE SUBMITTED IT HAVE DECLARED THAT IT MAY BE A MALICIOUS FORGERY. IN EITHER CASE IT SERVES AS A POIGNANT REMINDER OF THE HARDSHIPS OF WAR AND THE LENGTHS TO WHICH DESPERATE MEN WILL GO TO ALLEVIATE THEM.

My first impulse, naturally, was to return them to Walker with some biting remark. But then it occurred to me that Elizabeth had been moaning faintly only that morning about the monotony of our meat ration. It seemed a long time since we had eaten anything but spam or brawn and a succulent roast pigeon would, I knew, please her immensely.

'Well – thank you, Walker,' I said civilly.

Just then the wireless came on. We had missed the main part of the news, about the big events going on in Europe, but the more humble events that the announcer now announced were quite riveting enough, thank you.

'... the mysterious drop in the number of pigeons in Trafalgar Square remains unexplained. The Home Secretary said that he saw no cause for alarm and promised a full investigation. In answer to a parliamentary question he said he felt it was unlikely that there was a link between this event and the fall in the population of apes on the rock of Gibraltar.'

At the end of this grim announcement a silence fell upon the men clustered in the bunker, a silence broken only by the drone of enemy aircraft and the steady crump crump of the ack-ack guns. Then Walker stammered:

'No, not the apes. I give you my word of honour I never touched one single ape.'

This was, of course, tantamount to an admission that he had been responsible for the disappearance of the pigeons. Even through my anger and sense of patriotic outrage – since it is known that the pigeons in Trafalgar Square are widely considered to be a symbol of Empire and England, just as the apes are on the rock of Gibraltar – I was conscious of feeling a stir of respect. A man who could spirit away dozens of pigeons from the very heart of London in wartime was clearly a man who might one day give the enemy cause to tremble. But clearly it was not desirable for me to enquire too closely into whatever nefarious schemes had been

BETTER POT-LUCK with Churchill today

THAN HUMBLE PIE under Hitler tomorrow

DON'T WASTE FOOD!

hatched and perpetrated in the very ranks of my platoon. Moreover, Elizabeth and I could not, in all conscience, feast upon a couple of symbols of empire. So I coldly handed the birds back to Walker.

I had given Wilson a few days leave in order to sort out whatever was bothering him. We'd left it that he'd turn up for Church Parade on the Sunday if he'd got his life back on an even keel by then. I felt it my duty to warn him not to turn up drunk, since a scandal was something the platoon could not afford. It would have given the vicar the excuse he'd long been seeking to have us banned from the Church Hall.

Wilson had given his word that he would be well turned-out and utterly sober, and I must admit that when he arrived at church he was certainly both of those things. He looked very smart in a well-pressed uniform and his eyes were clear. He was a little behind me in the queue for hymn books being doled out by Private Frazer, and I smiled pleasantly at him and indicated the pew where I'd be sitting. I naturally expected him to join me there but he seemed to take rather a long time and I turned round to see what had become of him. To my utter amazement I saw him locked in an embrace with a beautiful young Wren. Right there in the church door, bold as brass. And when they'd concluded their torrid encounter, to their mutual satisfaction no doubt, the two lovebirds gazed long into each other's eyes and then the lovely dark-haired girl picked up a suitcase and departed, presumably in the direction of the station.

I must say I was utterly flabbergasted. Hints that Wilson had a soft spot for the ladies had often reached me, especially from young Pike, who

FROM JONES' EXPRESSION, AS HE DELICATELY FINGERS HIS ORGAN, WE SENSE THAT HE IS LOST IN ROMANTIC DREAMS – PERHAPS OF THE LADY IN WHOSE HONOUR HE ORIGINALLY MASTERED 'ONWARD CHRISTIAN SOLDIERS'.

gave the impression that Wilson's frequent visits to his mother's house did not always terminate at a seemly hour. But this flaunting of a new mistress – and one young enough to be his own daughter – in the hallowed precincts of the church seemed to take the biscuit.

I determined to have it out with Wilson as soon as church parade was over and warn him that if he wished to play the Lothario he would have to do it in some other platoon. Then I reflected that his new paramour had probably been on her way out of Walmington and possibly also out of the amorous sergeant's life. I further reflected that Wilson was loyal and reliable and that it was hard to see where I could find another man with those qualities, and thus the potential for promotion to sergeant, in the platoon. So I decided that I would let the matter rest and see if there were any repercussions in the future. If any repercussions do occur I'll report them in a future entry in this log, but if no repercussions crop up you can assume that Wilson has gone back to his stable relationship with Mrs Pike, assuming, of course, that he ever had a stable relationship with Mrs Pike which is, of course, pure speculation in the first place and largely the result of that stupid boy always calling him Uncle Arthur.

Anyway Uncle Ar– that is Sergeant Wilson did ultimately join me in my pew and we settled down to the service. I naturally assumed that Wilson's display of naked lust, which would not have disgraced a Marseilles bordello, was the last of the extraordinary events that would occur during the service. How wrong I was!

Some way through the service the vicar called for 'Onward, Christian Soldiers' and, as previously arranged, Corporal Jones rose to play it on the organ. As he edged his way past us and on down the aisle, Private Walker, looking rather green, said:

'Where's 'e going?'

He gazed after Jones as a condemned man might have gazed at an approaching firing squad. Then he rose and started shuffling hastily along the pew towards the central aisle. But when he reached me I asked pointedly:

'Where are you going, Walker?'

'Well – er – you see, Captain Mainwaring – I thought I'd – I'd help with the collection.'

'Go back to your place,' I ordered him.

For a moment I thought he would disobey this direct command but,

A MAIDEN LOVED
AN IDLE WORD
A COMRADE LOST
AND ADOLF SERVED

realising that it would be mutiny, he sighed deeply, turned and went back to his place. It was not long before the reason for his anxiety was made clear.

Jones started playing, but very little sound came out of the organ. The verger was struggling to turn the handle of the bellows and he was clearly finding it a bit of a hard task. I saw Jones say something to him and gathered it was an exhortation to work harder. The verger toiled to the maximum of his strength. A feeble note sounded and suddenly, with a soft 'thwuck', not unlike the sound made by a 2-inch mortar, a dressed pigeon shot into the air and landed on the organ. I had to applaud Jones's spirit. Although a cloud of feathers rose like a smoke screen from the bird, Jones valiantly struggled on. Soon there were three more 'thwucks', and three more pigeons shot out of organ

AN EXTRAORDINARY PICTURE, DOUBTLESS TAKEN BY A PARISHIONER, OF THE VICAR'S DISMAY AT THE 'PIGEON BOMBARDMENT'.

pipes and landed in the congregation. And after that the barrage increased until the civilians were fleeing, my men were putting on their steel helmets and the vicar was having what looked like a nervous breakdown.

So there you have it. Just an ordinary week in the life of a Home Guard commander. Was Wilson two-timing, as I believe the Yanks put it, Mrs Pike? Was Walker flagrantly exploiting symbols of empire for gain? And if so why did he stuff them in the church's organ pipes? I shall say at once: I have no idea as to the answer to these questions. Furthermore, I am glad that I have no idea. There can be wisdom in ignorance. In the regular army it would have been essential to get to the bottom of these questions in order to maintain discipline. But in a Home Guard unit, where every man and officer is not just a comrade-in-arms but a fellow citizen, there are stones which are best left unexplored, as the old saying has it. As long as my men remain a ruthless fighting force, ready at a moment's notice to repel the Hun invader, their

private lives are their own. I will not intrude upon them.

✦ ❬ ❬ ◈ ❭ ❭ ✦

IT IS NOT OFTEN that an editor can take over the role of story-teller but in this instance my researches enable me to do so. I am happy to be able to reveal the true story of my Uncle Arthur's beautiful Wren 'girl-friend'.

After the departure of the mysterious 'beautiful Wren', Arthur Wilson sat down and, his heart brimming over, penned a letter to my father. But, as I have since ascertained, my father was unaware of the antecedents of this letter – one of the reasons why he remained baffled to the end of his life by his poor brother's opting for obscurity – and in the event Uncle Arthur must have decided against sending his *cri de coeur*. He screwed it up and threw it into the wastepaper basket.

How it found its way from Uncle Arthur's wastepaper basket into Captain Mainwaring's document collection must remain a subject of conjecture. Might it be that the prudent bank manager and Home Guard commander, ever vigilant for the security both of the realm and his bank, made a practice of shuffling through the rubbish for anything relevant to these two goals? I hesitate to venture an opinion but am eternally grateful that he did so. Had he not the world might have been deprived forever of the following touching document, some parts of which are missing but which, in this editor's opinion, is no less poignant for that.

> *. . . Oh, Barney, Barney what a terrible – well – mess I've made of things. Oh what a tangled web we weave when – you know the thing, I'm sure. By that Scotch poet – the one who wrote about mice eating haggis & so forth. Anyway, what I'm trying to say is, if only I could undo it all and start again with a clean slate. But it's not possible, you see. The moving finger just will keep on writing, as that Persian Johnny put it. I don't know*

*why poetry keeps coming into my head. The last few days
have been a nightmare, Barney. Yes, but a nightmare with
glorious sunny spells. I seem to have caught the bug too.
Forgive me if I get a little romantic, but how would you feel if
your daughter turned up after fifteen years? I wish you could
have seen her Barney, in her Wren's uniform, a bonny girl with
a trim figure and dark hair. She looked very like her mother
the last time I saw her. Of course, you never met Beverley,
Barney. I knew I'd disgraced myself in the eyes of the family
but so help me there was nothing I could do about it. I was
passion's pawn. One glimpse of Beverley at that hunt ball and
I went right off my bean. Well, I kept it secret from you all and
we did the classic thing, eloped and a year later little Lucinda
was born and a sweet baby she was. We knew three glorious
years of happiness and then Beverley met that bounder,
Ponson—, no I won't mention his name. He may still be alive
although he was rotten with malaria.*

*She went off with him and they lived in some slum in
Limehouse above an opium den. When I found out I insisted
on making regular contributions. And when Lucy was old
enough, I put her through school, ending up with Roedean.
Took every penny of family money that came my way but it's
been worth it, Barney. She's grown up into a fine young lady
with that certain patina you only acquire at the very best
schools. One wouldn't be ashamed of her at a royal garden
party – so cool and poised and with that natural grace that
only comes from being born of really good stock.*

*Perhaps after this wretched war is over we'll meet again but
she's at present under starter's orders for Malta. Of course her
presence in town caused the most absurd mix-ups. In the first
place, Mavis – that is a woman of the village I'm slightly
acquainted with – positively leaped to the wrong conclusion
and threw a ch–...*

But the rest of this most moving missive is lost, gnawed away by mice it would appear. The reader will easily imagine its effect on me when I first perused it. So many things fell into place that had puzzled me since childhood. My uncle's self-imposed exile had not, I perceived, been merely an eccentric whim but a kind of penitential withdrawal from the world by a man who had loved 'not wisely but too well'. It might not be too fanciful to suggest that, for my Uncle Arthur, Walmington-on-Sea had been the spiritual equivalent of some blistering fort in the Sahara and his life as chief clerk at the bank and latterly sergeant in the local Home Guard platoon not very different from a long stretch of service in the French Foreign Legion. But I fear personal emotion is not the most suitable tool for the social historian. So let us pass on to more robust matters.

How and why did Private Walker manage to appropriate a substantial proportion of the pigeon population of Trafalgar Square? The first part of the question is soon answered. It is contained in a terse jotting in the diary that Corporal Jones kept throughout his adult life. I should explain that Corporal Jones, although usually presented by Captain Mainwairing as a verbose old idiot, displays quite a different 'image' (to use a current 'buzz word') of himself in his personal diary. This is composed of very short entries, few of them more than a dozen words long, in which the gruff soldier, rather than the garrulous old butcher, is dominant. During his early Sudan days, for example, we get abundant entries of the kind: 'Chased Fuzzy-Wuzzies with bayonet'; 'Very hot again – sweated a lot'; 'Attacked Mad Son of Mad

ALL THE ACCUMULATED REMORSE OF A LIFETIME IS SURELY ETCHED ON THE OLD WARRIOR'S FACE AS HE ASKS HIMSELF WHETHER THE CONSOLATION OFFERED BY A 'VILLAGE WOMAN CALLED MAVIS' CAN REALLY COMPENSATE HIM FOR THE LOST SPLENDOURS OF HIS RIGHTFUL PLACE IN THE WORLD.

A FRIENDLY NOTE TO ALL MY CUSTOMERS. LADIES, PLEASE DO NOT ASK FOR EXTRA MEAT AS A REFUSAL MAY LOSE ME A GOOD CUSTOMER.

Why does Mrs. Fox always seem to have plenty of off-the-ration sausages and dripping? Can there be a connection between her good fortune and the fact that she can often be seen flitting about the alley beside P. Jones' shop late at night? Perhaps someone should inform the Ministry of Food in London about this carry-on unless it stops forthwith.

A REMARKABLE STUDY OF TORMENTED CONSCIENCE. CORPORAL JONES, WHO HAS APPARENTLY RETAINED SOME OF WALKER'S ILL-GOTTEN PIGEONS, IS TORN BETWEEN HIS DUTY TO HIS MEAT-STARVED CLIENTS AND HIS REPUGNANCE AT DEALING IN THE 'WINGED SYMBOLS OF EMPIRE'.

Mahdi'. But the entry relevant to the mysterious matter of the pigeons is from 8 June 1942 and reads simply: 'Desperate for off-ration meat. Joe promises to help.'

So that is the motivation behind Walker's confiscation of the winged symbols of liberty, the graceful doves of Trafalgar Square, beloved of generations of nut-scattering children. But how, in the very citadel of empire, almost within range, as it were, of the great Churchill's frowning disapproval, had Walker succeeded in spiriting away the airy multitude? Alas, we shall probably never know.

IF THE EPISODE I have just included goes a long way towards humanising the steely commander of the Walmington-on-Sea Home Guard platoon, then the next one brings him fully into the human arena. No one who reads the following passionate account could fail to accord this British officer high status in the ranks of those who have bared their souls to the influence of love, who have revealed themselves – no matter how formidable as men of action – as heroes too of the human heart. I could, echoing Mark Antony's great oration in Shakespeare's *Julius Caesar*, cry: 'If you have tears, prepare to shed them now ...'. But I will make no sensational appeals. I will only express the personal view that the words which follow struck this particular reader as amongst the most poignant he has ever seen on a page and that he emerged from them with a new understanding of man's capacity for both love and sacrifice.

◆ ⟨ ⟨ ◆ ⟩ ⟩ ◆

YES, WELL BY now you'll be getting some idea of what this log is all about. It's about spit and polish for one thing, about recruiting training and then maintaining a first-rate, fully-equipped and operational fighting force. Its pages necessarily reek of combat. It's not the place for sighs and tender phrases. Nor is it the place for slush and romance. So why am I going to tell you about what can only, I suppose, be called a love affair? I'll tell you why. Because it is sometimes forgotten that a Home Guard officer, or any other kind for that matter, is also a man with all the frailties and giddy desires of any other man. He is not – not all the time anyway – a creature of steel with a brain like a calculating machine. Not a bit of it. His eyes know what it is to shed salt tears. His heart had been known to heave in his chest. And the point I'm getting at is that the ordinary weak human being may, and sometimes does, influence the stern officer who shares the same body. That fact makes it a suitable – indeed a necessary – subject for my log. So just for this one week forget the clash of steel and the smoke of battle. Forget the grim foe con-

WOMEN AT WAR. WHO CAN SAY IF THE FRUGAL HOUSEWIVES, COLLECTING OLD BONES AND SIMILAR RUBBISH WITH WHICH TO SMITE HITLER, WERE NOT MAKING A LARGER CONTRIBUTION TOWARDS ULTIMATE VICTORY THAN THE SCANTILY CLAD DAMSELS CLEARLY READY TO MAKE ANY REASONABLE SACRIFICE TO ENCOURAGE THE WAR EFFORT?

"UP HOUSEWIVES AND AT 'EM!"

THERE ARE WAR WEAPONS in your household waste—get them out! Be a miser with paper, metal, bones.* Save every scrap—the country needs them urgently. Keep them separate and put them by your dustbin every collection day.

Also put out waste food if this is collected in your district.

PUT THEM OUT CAREFULLY
Follow the instruction

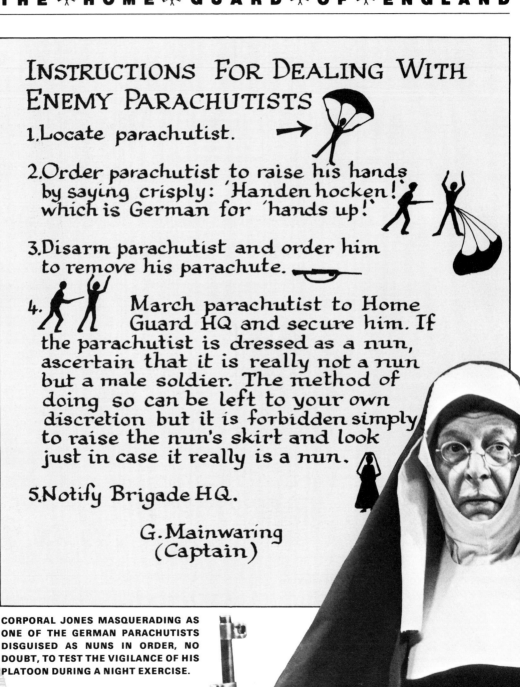

INSTRUCTIONS FOR DEALING WITH ENEMY PARACHUTISTS

1. Locate parachutist.

2. Order parachutist to raise his hands by saying crisply: 'Handen hocken!' which is German for 'hands up!'

3. Disarm parachutist and order him to remove his parachute.

4. March parachutist to Home Guard HQ and secure him. If the parachutist is dressed as a nun, ascertain that it is really not a nun but a male soldier. The method of doing so can be left to your own discretion but it is forbidden simply to raise the nun's skirt and look just in case it really is a nun.

5. Notify Brigade HQ.

G. Mainwaring
(Captain)

CORPORAL JONES MASQUERADING AS ONE OF THE GERMAN PARACHUTISTS DISGUISED AS NUNS IN ORDER, NO DOUBT, TO TEST THE VIGILANCE OF HIS PLATOON DURING A NIGHT EXERCISE.

fronting us from across the channel. Forget the black dive-bombers screaming down to spit their load of death onto our fields and cities. And let an old soldier – officer actually – guide you on a rare journey into the human heart.

In order to trace the origins of this tragic little tale I must take you back a couple of months to a parade I held in the Church Hall. Nothing special about it – our routine Saturday night arms drill. But when the drill was over and Jones had finally ceased spinning and staggering about and been helped back to his feet, I addressed the platoon with a little idea that had been forming in my mind.

'Men,' I began, 'we are fighting an all-out war. The old gentlemanly distinctions have been lost. When bombers are overhead we are all soldiers whether in uniform or not. Even more important, women for the first time find themselves in the front line. Now the fact is that I have recently been approached by several of the brave women of Walmington-on-Sea. They have asked if there isn't a place for them too in our fight against the common foe?'

'Well there's always –' began Walker, grinning suggestively.

'That's quite enough, Walker,' I silenced him. 'And to resume, an auxiliary force of women could be of immense help to us. They could, for example, take over much of the paperwork and the making of tea and cocoa and – other things to eat and drink. Now have any of you any other suggestions as to how a women's branch could be of use to this platoon?'

'Buttons, sir,' called Frazer eagerly.

For a moment I thought he was trying his hand at Walker's type of smut. But, giving him the benefit of the doubt, I asked politely:

'I beg your pardon?'

'Buttons, sir. They could sew on buttons.'

I nodded in satisfaction. 'Precisely. A very good point. Make a note of that, would you, Sergeant Wilson?'

The sergeant, a trifle lethargically I felt, withdrew a pencil and note-pad from his breast pocket as he sighed: 'Yes, of course, sir. Excellent idea.'

Godfrey, who had been showing a familiar tendency to shuffle a trifle uneasily on the spot and gaze wistfully towards the door leading to the conveniences, made a suggestion.

'My sister is very good at sewing, sir. Dolly does very beautiful petit point although she does need someone to thread the needle for her.' I nodded judiciously. 'I'll make a mental note of that,

Godfrey. Although I'm not really sure that there'll be much need for petit point when the balloon goes up.'

At this point young Pike, hopping from foot to foot like a nervous schoolboy, called 'sir' and was given permission to speak.

'There's a new girl at the sweet shop,' he informed us. 'She's very obliging.'

Inevitably, I suppose, Walker put his oar in.

'Just what I 'ad in mind – comforts for the . . .'

But I interrupted him firmly. 'We don't want any more of that talk, Walker.'

Frazer licked his lips while his huge eyes rolled in concentration. Then he offered: 'There's a lassie works for the Gaslight and Coke Company. She's a good girl with a firm body and big strong thighs.'

Jones contributed: 'They're very strong – the ones with big thighs.'

Wondering why the discussion

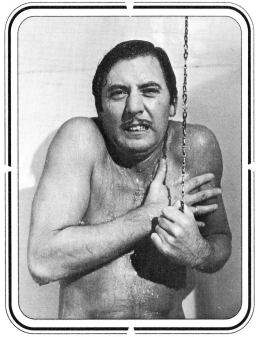

AFTER ONE TOO MANY OF WALKER'S TORRID JOKES, MAINWARING HAS CLEARLY ORDERED THE BAWDY SOLDIER TO 'TAKE A COLD SHOWER AND COOL OFF THAT WAY'.

seemed to keep taking this unfortunate direction, I hurriedly continued.

'Anyway, I'm sure that between us we can find enough of the right sort. So I want you all to bring suitable recruits along to our next parade. Properly trained, these women will release us – the front-line troops – so that we can grapple with the enemy.'

'Doesn't seem likely,' Walker sniggered, 'that Taffy and Jones will have much energy left after grappling with all those big thighs.'

'I shan't tell you again, Walker,' I rebuked him in an icy tone. The man looked abashed and I dismissed the parade.

A week later I entered my office where Wilson was at work on Part 2 orders.

'Ah, good evening, Wilson,' I said cordially. 'There seems to be a good number of women recruits out there.'

Wilson nodded and rose from the desk to make way for me. 'Yes, sir, the men have brought a surprising number along.'

'Right,' I said, seating myself. 'Let's have them in – one at a time.'

Wilson departed and a moment later returned escorting Corporal Jones and Mrs Fox, a plump lady with a slightly too breezy manner for my taste and a tendency to laugh wildly. I have sometimes seen her at functions with Corporal Jones. Wilson was speaking to Mrs Fox as they entered.

'What an awfully humid day it's been,' he murmured.

'Yes, hasn't it?' said Mrs Fox, giggling as if he'd made a witty remark.

'Still,' purred Wilson, 'you're looking marvellously cool.' Then he addressed me – and about time too. 'This is Mrs Fox, sir.'

I nodded as I rose and, as an officer should, saluted. 'Yes, we have met before. How do you do, Mrs Fox.'

'Nicely, thank you,' she giggled, for no reason that I could fathom.

Jones piped up. 'She's one of my best customers, sir. I think you will find she will give every satisfaction.'

'Thank you, Jones,' I said distantly.

'By jove, how rude of me!' Wilson abruptly exclaimed. 'I'm letting you stand.'

Wilson reached for a chair behind him and placed it behind Mrs Fox. 'Do sit down, Mrs Fox. And is there anything we can get you? Would you like a nice cup of tea or something?'

Mrs Fox giggled again and tossed her head. 'Oh, don't trouble,' she exclaimed with what I would call a decidedly roguish manner.

'But it's no trouble,' Wilson assured her, sounding like some Regency buck. 'The kettle's on. It won't take a moment.'

Clearly this farce had to be terminated. I rose and moved to the door of my office, saying: 'Wilson, I'd like a word with you outside, please.'

1. Hold your breath. Put on mask wherever you are. Close window.

The sergeant naturally had no option but to follow me. Once outside my office, and in a low voice because I had no wish to humiliate him in front of the men, I said: 'Wilson, I know you are something of a lady's man but these women are going to be subject to discipline like the rest of our force. Let's start as we mean to go on, shall we?'

Wilson gave a little smile and demurred. 'But surely we can be polite, sir?'

'Of course, but that doesn't mean we have to have all this Jack Buchanan stuff. Let's just stick to the business in hand, if you don't mind.'

'Whatever you say, sir.'

I nodded and we returned to my office and resumed enlisting Mrs Fox.

'Sorry for the interruption,' I apologised to her. 'Now, let's see – the name is Fox. What about your Christian name!'

'Marcia.'

At this, Wilson exclaimed, 'What a pretty name!'

Inevitably I suppose, Mrs Fox gave one of her boisterous giggles and asked flirtatiously, 'Do you think so?'

'It's one of my favourites,' said the Sergeant. 'I once knew a – '

'Wilson!' I said sharply and, with an apologetic look, he fell silent once more. Mrs Fox handed me a card and explained.

'That's my address.' She then glanced about and, blushing a little, said softly, 'I've written my age on the bottom.'

'Thank you,' I said, being at a loss to know what else to say.

'Occupation?' I continued.

'Widow,' said Mrs Fox, demurely for the first time.

'Is that an occupation?' I asked in genuine perplexity.

'In Mrs Fox's case,' contributed Wilson in a voice that was oozing gallantry, 'I would say it was almost a calling.'

'Wilson!' I exclaimed in my sternest voice thus far. He looked deeply abashed. Perhaps to help him over the bumpy patch Jones said in a garbled kind of way:

'Mrs Fox is a very fine lady, sir, and a most understanding and female kind of warm-looking person.'

'Yes, of course,' I agreed doubtfully, and then to Mrs Fox, 'Would you like to join us?'

With a sly little giggle, she said: 'I didn't know you'd come apart.'

❦ A POEM FOR AMY ❦
by Frank Pike

Roses are red, violets are blue
Please tell me, Amy,
That you will be true.
Because I love you.

Parsnips are white, cabbage is green
You're the prettiest girl
That I've ever seen.
And that's something I mean.

Apples are green, peaches are orange,
Last night when I kissed you,
I felt a bit like a lozenge
Or if I'd got the mange.

No that doesn't sound good. Try again.
Apples are green, bananas are yellow,
Last night when I kissed you,
I felt very mellow
And a very lucky fellow. ❦

"I'll give you kissing at your age! You stupid boy! There'll be time enough for girls when you've got settled in some job! If you want to know where all this skirt-chasing gets you, just look at your fa – your Uncle Arthur. He couldn't wait for the right woman to come along and that's why he's so grey and miserable. Do you want to be like him? No more of it, Frank!"

"Of course there's no harm in your knowing!"

CARELESS TALK COSTS LIVES

This daft utterance produced a perfect explosion of mirth from Wilson. 'What an awfully good quip. Don't you think so, sir?'

Realising that there was something about the proximity of a female that apparently turned Wilson's brains to porridge, I contented myself with sighing. To Mrs Fox, I said: 'I assume that's an affirmative, Mrs Fox. I'll put your name down. Could we have the next lady, please, Wilson?'

Wilson stepped out into the church hall and returned a moment or two later with Private Pike and a thin and, frankly, rather mousy-looking girl. Pike piped up at once.

'This is the young lady I was telling you about, sir. Amy Samways.'

I wrote the name down carefully while Wilson elaborated.

'You may remember, sir – this is the girl that is supposed to be very obliging.'

I shot him a sharp look and said meaningfully, 'Thank you, Wilson.'

Then I interrogated Miss Samways – a protracted and irritating process, because the young lady proved to have a very tiny voice. In fact, she was utterly inaudible. I would say to her: 'Address, please, Miss Samways?'

Then her lips moved but no sound emerged. I asked her if she'd be so good as to repeat it and the same thing happened. Then Pike, Wilson and I all looked at each other in baffled bewilderment. The question about the address was not too difficult to solve because Pike, it turned out, knew it and gave it to us: 27, Jutland Drive. But that's about all we were able to find out for certain. Still, in the end we enrolled her. It struck me that she might be effective as the guardian of the platoon secrets. Jerry would never get a thing out of that girl.

I asked for the next lady and Wilson went out and returned with Walker and a rather bold-looking girl who was chewing gum. This is a habit which has never commended itself to me. I know that the Yanks insist that it is very good for the teeth, but I find it disconcerting to try and hold a conversation with someone who is apparently munching thin air. In this case, I also had to ask myself where the young lady might have acquired the chewing gum but then, of course, I recalled that Walker managed to lay his hands on a surprising variety of scarce items.

Walker grinned in the rather over-familiar manner he sometimes displays and said: 'This is Edith Parrish, Mr Mainwaring. She's – er – you could say she's a good friend of mine. We have a lot of the same tastes and we both especially like making –'

'That's quite enough, Walker.' I silenced him. Then I smiled encouragingly at the young muncher – lady. 'Now Miss Parrish, do you have an occupation?'

In a voice that could hardly be described as aristocratic, she nodded and said: 'Yeah – I'm an usherette.'

Unnecessarily, Walker chimed in. 'That's just what she is – at the Tivoli Cinema – you know, with a torch.'

'Quite, Walker. Well then, Miss Parrish, I expect you see a lot of pictures?'

A faint, cynical smile appeared on her brassy, but not unattractive, features. She nodded. 'Yeah – an' I see a lot of other things an' all.'

Again Walker chipped in. 'Incidentally, Mr Mainwaring, any time you want to see a film at the Tivoli just knock three times on the fire exit round the side alley and Edie here will see you alright. Won't you, darlin'?'

'Don't mind,' she said, chewing lustily and looking me up and down in a faintly disturbing manner.

I nodded distantly and remarked: 'Yes, well I don't think I shall be taking advantage of your hospitality, Miss Parrish. May I ask, where do you live?'

She sniffed suspiciously and replied: 'Down Berwick Road – 35, but I live with my dad and he's six foot three – so you needn't get any ideas.'

This astonishing effrontery was nearly enough to induce me to dismiss the young woman without further ado. But then I reflected that she might still be capable of playing a useful role in the women's branch of our Home Guard unit and I enrolled her, albeit reluctantly.

So the evening wore on and I gradually built up a small, but valuable, auxiliary branch of our platoon. But I have to confess that I was relieved when the last applicant had been signed on and I was able to say to Wilson: 'Right, sergeant, dismiss the men and you can leave yourself once you've done so.'

'Thank you, sir,' smiled Wilson, saluting lethargically.

A little while later I heard the clump of ammunition boots across the wooden floor and then silence. I sighed and began to gather up my papers preparatory to leaving myself. There was a discreet knock at the door. Wondering who it could be, I called 'Come in.'

Through the door came – well, how can I put it? It would not be strictly

A REAL LIFE SCENE SO POIGNANT AND DRAMATIC THAT IT COULD EASILY BE FROM A FILM. DIS-
TRAUGHT AT THE NEWS THAT MRS FOX'S HOMEWARD-BOUND TRAIN HAS BEEN MACHINE-GUNNED,
CORPORAL JONES ATTEMPTS TO DROWN HIS GRIEF. HE IS RESTRAINED BY HIS CONCERNED
COMRADES. MERCIFULLY THERE IS A HAPPY ENDING TO THIS DESPERATE STORY – MRS FOX WAS
LATER FOUND TO HAVE TAKEN A LATER TRAIN.

true to say an angel. But I have to admit that she looked like that to me. Of course she was really a woman but what a very attractive one. Not a bit like the – how can I put this? – somewhat coarser girls and women I had been interviewing. This lady was not, admittedly, in the first flush of youth but she was nonetheless very lovely. She had brown hair and a trim figure and she was dressed with great style and class. You could tell that she patronised the best shops. I was not surprised to discover that her voice had a certain ring of elegance and breeding. Her smile was friendly but not in the least bold. I was quite bowled over – but naturally I concealed it beneath the brusque manner appropriate to a fighting officer.

'Captain Mainwaring?' she asked.

I nodded. 'That's right.'

'I've heard you need women helpers for the Home Guard – is that right?'

'Yes, yes, quite correct. Do sit down. Do you know, your face seems familiar. Could I have seen you at the Golf Club?'

She shook her head sorrowfully, or so it seemed to me. She gave me another friendly smile.

'No,' she explained, 'I've not been in Walmington long. I had to bring my mother away from London – because of the bombing. Oh, I'd sooner have stayed in town. True, I couldn't have helped much but just being there would have shown that wretched little Hitler that we're not going to give in.'

I gazed at her in admiration and respect. 'By jove,' I exclaimed. 'That's the sort of talk I like to hear.'

For what seemed to me quite a long moment our eyes remained in close contact. Can do funny things to a chap, that sort of close eye contact. I could feel something remarkably like a refreshing breeze rippling across my scalp, just as you get sometimes on early morning exercises with the sun just coming up along the coast and perhaps a skein of wild duck honking overhead. You know the kind of thing: an awareness of something very precious that you'd give anything to ki– to protect. Clearing my throat gruffly, and in my most impersonal and official tone of voice, I asked: 'Now then, could I have your name?'

'Gray. Fiona Gray.'

Despite myself, I gave a kind of snort of enthusiasm.

'Fiona,' I said and I wouldn't swear a faint note of reverence hadn't crept into my voice. 'What a pretty name.'

'Thank you,' she said sweetly.

'Erm – occupation?'

'Well – ,' she appeared to ponder for a moment. 'Widow, I suppose – if you can call that an occupation.'

'In your case,' I exclaimed fervently, 'I would have to say it was almost a calling.'

As I said this I could not help frowning for it seemed to me that my remark was the very echo of something I had read or heard recently. But I could not bring it to mind.

I had soon obtained all the necessary remaining particulars. Then I said:

'I think that's about it then. I'll look forward to seeing you tomorrow night. We usually parade at about seven o'clock.'

She nodded enthusiastically. 'Oh, I can't wait to start. At the moment my life consists of morning coffee at Ann's Pantry and making the dahlias grow.'

'I'm very fond of dahlias,' I exclaimed.

'Really? Do you grow them too?'

I shook my head mournfully. 'No … no, unfortunately. My wife says they attract earwigs.'

'Well, she's right, of course. But it's still a pity.'

At this point Mrs Gray paused and I had the feeling that she was trying to decide whether or not to say something that was on her mind. How right I was. The next moment, in a soft, caressing voice, she asked: 'Captain Mainwaring, may I say something awfully personal?'

'Of course you may.'

'Do you always wear spectacles?'

I was a trifle nonplussed by this question – couldn't see quite what she was getting at. I nodded.

'Yes, I do – actually.'

With a smile to soften what might have seemed an impertinent request, she asked gently: 'Would you take them off for a moment?'

I have to admit I felt a kind of warmth in my cheeks after she'd asked this and I realised that I was blushing. I think the thing was no one had shown the slightest interest in my appearance since – well, I suppose since Elizabeth and I were courting and then it was only when Elizabeth asked me if I had all my own teeth. Feeling a bit of a fool but pleased nonetheless, I took off

DO YOU WANT SOME OF MY BRAWN?

EACH BOOK WILL BE ENTITLED TO RECEIVE THREE OUNCES OF IT DURING THE FORTHCOMING RATION PERIOD. I MAY ALSO HAVE SOME SPARE SAUSAGES.

M. Jones

SHORTAGES WERE THE BANE OF CIVILIAN LIFE. BUT EVEN UNDER THE SUSPICIOUS GAZE OF WALMINGTON'S HOUSEWIVES, CORPORAL JONES USUALLY MANAGED TO SLIP AN EXTRA SAUSAGE OR TWO TO HIS BELOVED MRS FOX.

my glasses. Fiona – but I suppose I should still be calling her Mrs Gray even after all that has passed between us – said:

'Oh, that's so much better. They cut off so much warmth – just as a fireguard takes away so much of the heat.'

I gazed at her in surprise. I'd never thought of it like that. 'I – I suppose you're right – I mean – well the thing is – '

'Oh you're still here, sir?' exclaimed Wilson, entering without knocking.

I could have strangled him. Instead I tried to put my glasses back on in a hurry, dropped them on my desk and then, unable to see clearly at that distance, had to scrabble around until I found them by touch and, when I had finally replaced them on my nose, was rewarded by the sight of Wilson smirking in amusement at me.

'Sergeant Wilson,' I said sternly. 'This is a new recruit. Mrs Fiona Gray.'

A slightly thunderstruck expression appeared on his face. 'Fiona!' he exclaimed. 'I say, what a pretty – '

'Why did you come back, Wilson?' I asked pointedly.

It seemed he'd forgotten his draft Part 2 orders. I handed them to him and saw him, very reluctantly it seemed to me, and with several backward glances and smiles in the direction of Mrs Gray, depart.

My God, but it's hard to put all this down in black and white. I've always been a down-to-earth sort of chap, plough a straight furrow, give a man a straight answer, dependable, typical bank manager you might say. But that's the whole point. If it could happen to me it could happen to anyone, and that's why I consider it my duty to write about it in this log. Don't be deceived by appearances. You see a chap like me with a few pips on his shoulders, out on the parade ground or encouraging his men in the thick of battle, and you think: that's a fighting soldier – nerves of steel – brain like an iron trap. And all the time the poor chap's doubled up inside about a woman. I'm absolutely sure that no one noticed anything untoward over the next few weeks. Sergeant Wilson, Corporal Jones, the humble rankers – to them I was the same dependable fearless officer that had always trained and led them. None of them suspected what turmoil was going on inside me, even when they saw me in Ann's Pantry.

'Ah, good morning, Mr Mainwaring,' said Mrs Gray in her enchanting voice the first day she encountered me there.

I looked up with, I have to admit, feigned surprise. 'Why, Mrs Gray,' I exclaimed. 'What an unexpected pleasure. Won't you join me?'

'I'd love to,' she said, and my heart, which had apparently knocked off work for some reason, started to beat again with great vigour.

She sat down at the table and, as she did so, said: 'I haven't seen you here before.'

I smiled dismissively. 'Oh, I come here from time to time, you know – when I can lift my nose from the grindstone.'

Just then the waitress arrived and we both ordered coffee. We sat for a little while in silence until she said:

'I do like this place.'

'So do I,' I assured her. 'You know, they used to do the most marvellous Devonshire teas here before the war.'

'With jam and cream?'

'Absolutely. Why I remember just after the first war –'

At this point I ground to a halt at the thought that I'd blown it pretty thoroughly. She would think I was some relic from a bygone age. I stole a glance at her but she was still smiling in an encouraging way. I got under way again.

MAINWARING'S BRAVERY WAS EQUAL TO ANY OCCASION. HERE WE SEE HIM TESTING A STEEL HELMET WHICH, IT WAS HOPED, WOULD PROVIDE PROTECTION AGAINST INCENDIARY BOMBS. THE PERFORATED CONE WAS INTENDED TO DISSIPATE THE HEAT OF SUCH A BOMB LANDING ON A SOLDIER'S HEAD. I HAVE NOT, ALAS, BEEN ABLE TO LOCATE MAINWARING'S REPORT ON THE INVENTION.

'Yes, it was just after I'd joined the Guildford branch of the bank. A chum and I borrowed a flivver and took a spin down here to Ann's Pantry, just for the Devonshire tea. When I got home I had the rough side of my governor's tongue I can tell you. He was under the impression that I'd toddled off with a bit of fluff.'

I breathed an inner sigh of relief. She'd realise from that account that I was right up to date with the latest slang.

'We had a lot of harmless fun, didn't we?' she said cheerfully. 'In the old days.'

'Of course we did,' I concurred. 'Mind you, we used to go the pace a bit now and then.'

I chuckled reminiscently although, to be utterly candid, I couldn't remember ever going the pace very much. Spent most of my time selling suits in my father's shop. I glanced up and this time my athletic heart did a kind of somersault and then stayed up in the air. Mrs Gray was smiling at me with an expression I can only call affectionate.

'You know,' she said, 'your whole face seems to light up when you laugh. I think you're a very jolly person at heart.'

I fancy I smiled gratefully at this observation and was just about to reply when a voice beside me said, in a tone of surprise:

'Oh – Captain Mainwaring!'

I looked up and beheld what appeared to be a huge baby gaping at me in astonishment. I squinted.

'Er – Godfrey, is it?'

'Yes, it is,' replied the immense infant. 'Have you lost your glasses, Captain Mainwaring?'

'No, no, just giving my eyes a rest.'

'I see. I've never seen you in here before, sir.'

'Well, I – pop in from time to time, you know.'

'I didn't know that. I have to hurry. I'm just on my way to the clinic.'

And Godfrey disappeared from my field of vision. I saw an amused expression on Mrs Gray's face.

'He's really a charming man,' I assured her. 'One of my most loyal soldiers.'

'They're a wonderful band of men,' she agreed.

'That's it,' I said proudly. 'Not a bad apple in the barrel.'

DINNER ME  4/8d

BROWN WINDSOR SOUP

OR

PILCHARD FILLETS

OR

SHREDDED CABBAGE SALAD

OR

TOAST SQUARES WITH MEAT PASTE

SPAM FRITTERS WITH BOILED POTATOES AND CABBAGE

OR

CRUSTY MACARONI CHEESE AND CABBAGE

OR

CAULIFLOWER CHEESE

OR

SAVOURY OMELETTE (MADE WITH POWDERED EGG) AND CABBAGE

OR

SNOEK CHIPS AND CABBAGE (WHEN FRYING FAT AVAILABLE)

JAM ROLY-POLY

OR

SPOTTED DICK

OR

APPLE TART WITH CUSTARD (WHEN AVAILABLE)

OR

CHEDDAR CHEESE WITH CRACKER

COFFEE (CAMP) 6d EXTRA

for vitality

eat greens

— 80 —

'Blimey,' exclaimed what I instantly recognised as the voice of Walker. 'Never seen you in 'ere before, Mr Mainwaring. Need any razor blades? Or what about some real French perfume for the lady? Pre-war stock. Smuggled over by General de Gaulle to finance the resistance. I can let you 'ave 'alf an ounce for –'

'No thanks, Walker,' I cut him off firmly.

''Ere! 'Ave you bust your specs? I can get you a new frame for only –'

'Walker! I haven't lost them. I'm just resting my eyes.'

'If I was sitting with what you're sitting with I'd want to see as much as possible.'

Horrified at the possibility that Mrs Gray would be embarrassed I began angrily: 'That's quite enough –'

''Ang about,' said Walker urgently. ''Ere comes the van with the sweet stuff. Just a small delivery I'm making.'

'Are you talking about black market sugar?'

'The thing is, Mr Mainwaring, if anyone asks you, you never seen me 'ere. And if anyone asks me, I'll return the favour.'

And the impudent rascal gave me a broad wink before hurrying through the swing doors into the back of the café. I noticed that Mrs Gray was gazing after him with an astonished look and I made the best of the situation.

'Heart of gold that man –' I proclaimed. 'Do anything for you. I don't think you've told me what part of London you come from?'

'Oh, just near –'

THIS PICTURE OF MAINWARING AT A FORMAL FUNCTION CLEARLY STEMS FROM THE PERIOD OF HIS LOVE FOR MRS GRAY. HAVING DISCARDED HIS SPECTACLES TO PLEASE HER, THE EXTREMELY MYOPIC CAPTAIN IS REDUCED TO FEELING HIS WAY AROUND.

'Hello, Mr Mainwaring,' interrupted a slightly quavery, rather high-pitched voice which I recognised at once as belonging to Lance-Corporal Jones. 'Don't often see you in 'ere.'

I sighed deeply and turned towards the voice. There were two people beside our table and, with difficulty, I recognised one of them as the corporal. The other was somewhat larger and by the fact that it was wearing a dress I identified it as belonging to a person of the female sex. Jones at once confirmed this supposition.

'This here is Mrs Prosser. Mrs Prosser, that gentleman there at the table with the lady that is not his wife and I don't know who she is is Captain Mainwaring, our very much esteemed and gentleman-like platoon commander.'

I had no option but to return the civility. 'How do you do –' I murmured towards the couple. 'And this is Mrs Gray.'

'How do you do,' said Mrs Prosser with a giggle not unlike that of Mrs Fox.

Jones spoke to his companion. 'Now you sit down over there, my dear, and I'll join you in just a moment.'

There was a pause while the lady apparently obeyed this instruction. Then Jones, in something of a stage whisper, explained: 'Mrs Prosser is only a very good friend of mine, sir, but there is nothing more to it than the eye can see if it happens to be looking in our direction, sir, if you understand me.'

'Perfectly,' I replied.

'For all that, I'd be grateful if you wouldn't tell Mrs Fox that you've seen me with Mrs Prosser, sir, because of the way some ladies do take it into their heads to jump towards false conclusions. All it is is that I give Mrs Prosser pieces of offal for her cat and she on her part keeps me company from time to time if you get my meaning, sir?'

'Yes, yes, Jones,' I said, trying to stem this tide of unwanted confidences.

'Very good of you, sir, and in return I shall refrain from mentioning to your wife that I –'

'Alright, Jones,' I silenced him in a stern tone of voice. 'I'll see you on parade tonight.'

'That you will, sir,' he returned briskly.

And to my great relief, he departed.

'I'm so sorry about all these interruptions,' I said apologetically to Mrs

"ABOUT TURN!"

Gray. 'I must say I was looking forward to a nice cup of coffee and a quiet chat.'

To my great delight, she replied, 'So was I.'

This gave me courage to admit something that I would not have thought, a little while before, that I was capable of admitting.

'Actually,' I said and I noted that my voice was not quite without a tremor as I said it. 'I only came here on the chance that I might meet you.'

She smiled in a kind of radiant way. I had the impression, just for a moment, that someone had switched on some extra lights. 'I'd rather hoped that was the reason,' she said.

I leaned forwards and placed one hand over hers.

'Fiona,' I began.

'Captain Mainwaring,' whined young Pike who had materialised beside our table.

'What is it, you stupid boy?' I asked crossly, letting go of Mrs Gray's hand.

'I won't tell you if you're rude,' he pouted. 'I didn't mean to interrupt your courting but –'

'What do you want, Pike?' I roared, causing several heads to turn at adjoining tables.

'Uncle Arthur – that is Mr Wilson says to tell you the bank inspectors have arrived and you're to come at once.'

I sighed deeply. 'Alright, Pike, I'll be along in a minute. You can go.'

'It's not my fault if I have to be piggy-in-the-middle. You should go somewhere private when you –'

'I said I'd be along soon, Pike. Now, go back to the bank.'

Grumbling under his breath the sulky young man departed. Feeling no end of a fool I looked up at Mrs Gray.

'I say, I'm –'

I stopped. It was a little hard to see without my glasses and I leaned forwards a little. There was no doubt about it. The enchanting woman was laughing quietly. She reached out and patted my hand. I just gazed at her in something like adoration for a moment and then I felt my own shoulders begin to heave slightly. In a moment we were both laughing for all we were worth.

After that, and for the whole month it lasted, I lived only for our meetings, brief though these were. It was a case of a sandwich at lunchtime behind a barn out past the village limits, a coffee at Ann's Pantry with half the platoon grinning and nudging in the background, a peck on the cheek behind the hat stand if we happened to meet by chance at some social gathering. How I longed simply to bundle her up in my arms and carry her off to some South Sea Island. But, of course, this was not possible. She could not leave her mother and I was sensible of the terrible effect it would have on Elizabeth if I eloped to Tahiti. Besides, wartime restrictions on travel meant we'd have been lucky to get as far as the Isle of Wight, never mind Tahiti. But perhaps the most compelling reason of all was duty. I was aware that I still had a role to play in the defence of the realm. Without me the Walmington-on-Sea platoon could hardly function as a front-line fighting unit and might even disintegrate completely. I knew that I could not desert my post, no matter what the tug on my besieged heart. But each time we met – and even more each time we parted – every atom of my being yearned towards Mrs Gray (that is, Fiona); and while performing my chores in the bank, which now seemed quite meaningless, my mind often reached out to her. I can assure you that it is devilishly difficult to talk about remortgaging a farm with a smelly old farmer when you are in the throes of a passionate love affair.

The women's auxiliary unit, I must confess, was not a great success. This was not the fault of the women, who performed their allotted tasks conscientiously, but because the men's discipline suffered. Quite astonishing the effect the proximity of a few women helpers had on them. From being disciplined soldiers, eager to grapple with the foe, they became something of a bawdy rabble, forever making coarse jokes and seeking opportunities to get closer to the ladies. I did my best to combat this tendency for a time. But I was naturally aware of the irony of a commander who was himself smitten with Cupid's dart to wean his own men away from women. So in the end, I enrolled three of the women as special helpers and disbanded the unit. The special helpers worked in the background and not actually during parades, and gradually discipline reasserted itself.

It was only last Wednesday, just four days ago, that the blow fell, and so raw still is the wound that I ask myself how I can bear to write about it. I suppose the answer must be: steely self-discipline.

I had mustered the men in the church hall and was about to give them

For Fiona

A soldier's and not a poet's hand
Wields this pen to say you're grand,
Fiona, who has come from where
To help me my heavy burden bear.
I would lay down my arms and flee
If only I could stay with thee.
But that can never be, you see,
I bear a heavy burden of command
To train my valiant fighting band,
Fiona who has come from where
To help me my heavy burden bear.
Fiona, I knew your heart was mine
Then in my life a light would shine
And we would find a way to-to-
And we - oh God I can't do it.

ROTTEN!

a talk on the use of the Mills bomb in winkling out machine-gun nests when Pike arrived late. Naturally, I rebuked him.

'You're late, Pike, for the second time this month. I simply cannot tolerate this slackness.'

The stupid boy pouted resentfully. 'Couldn't help it, Mr Mainwaring. I had to help Mrs Gray.'

Naturally at this I pricked up my ears. 'Help Mrs Gray to do what?' I asked.

'Carry her suitcases. She had these two big suitcases and she had to keep putting them down because they were so heavy. So I volunteered to help because I'm a courtesy scout, second class.'

'Yes, yes,' I said impatiently, aware of a constriction in my chest. 'But

PRIVATE PIKE WAS CERTAINLY NOT AS STUPID AS MAINWARING MAINTAINED, BUT IT IS A LITTLE HARD TO UNDERSTAND WHY HE COULD NOT HAVE SKIRTED THIS MUDDY PATCH RATHER THAN GRIMLY MARCHING THROUGH IT.

where did you help her to carry these cases?'

'To the station. She's taking the train to London. I think you should be pleased that I have chivalrous instincts, Mr Mainwaring.'

'We'll say no more about it, Pike,' I assured the youth, but even as I did so my eyes moved to the wall clock. I saw that the time was nearly half-past seven. The next London train would be the seven fifty-nine. It might be just possible to reach the station before then, and the train was, in any case, sometimes late. I turned to Wilson.

'Something very urgent has come up, sergeant,' I informed him, oblivious of what he might think. 'Take over the parade. I'll be back later if it's at all possible.'

'Yes, of course, sir,' said Wilson and I must say it seemed to me that there was a note of genuine solicitude in his voice.

I cast dignity to the winds. I ran through the streets, for the first quarter of a mile or so anyway, and then, a little out of breath, I slowed to a fast walk. By the time I entered the station, just five minutes before the train was due, I was panting hard. But I forced myself on and as soon as I had bought my platform ticket and pushed through the swing doors onto the dark platform I saw her. She was in the waiting room, seated at one of the tables, sipping tea. Without ceremony I entered and went to her table. I seated myself.

'You didn't tell me you were going,' I said quietly.

'I thought it was best not to,' she returned. 'I suppose Pike told you?'

'Yes.'

'I was afraid he would. Oh I wish the train had been early.'

'But you're coming back? Your mother's still here?'

'No, she's not, George. She missed London and now that the raids are so much better she's gone home.'

'So you'd have just – just stolen away – without even a goodbye?'

'For both our sakes, George. It would have been best.'

'But I don't think I can bear it. I just live from one of our meetings to the next.'

'And I'm the same. But people have begun talking.'

'Damn their talk!'

'And there's your wife –'

'People won't say anything to her. She's not been out of the house since Munich.'

THE ⚔ HOM

THESE PHOTOGRAPHS MAY WELL CHART THE COURSE OF THE WOMEN'S AUXILIARY UNIT. ON THE LEFT CAPTAIN MAINWARING STANDS PROUDLY BEFORE A SPRUCE AND DISCIPLINED BODY OF WOMEN. ON THE RIGHT, POSSIBLY TAKEN WEEKS OR MONTHS LATER, THE ROT HAS SET IN AND THE PLATOON IS CLEARLY DECLINING INTO A GIRL-OBSESSED RABBLE.

IS YOUR JOURNEY REALLY NECESSARY?

RAILWAY EXECUTIVE COMMITTEE

'HEARTBREAK HALLS' WAS A POPULAR WARTIME TERM FOR RAILWAY STATIONS WHERE SO MANY TEARS WERE SHED. IT WAS ONLY TRUE HEROS, LIKE MAINWARING, WHO COULD BIND THEIR BREAK-ING HEARTS WITH HOOPS OF STEEL AND RETURN AT ONCE TO THEIR POSTS.

Then I heard it, the rumble of the approaching train. I reached forwards and seized her hand.

'Fiona, I beg you – and I've never begged anyone for anything before in my life – don't take that train.'

'I must. There's no future for us, George. Two little people just don't matter in this terrible war –'

'But where can I reach you? When will I see you again?'

'Perhaps – if we both survive – perhaps after the war – but it would be better if we just forgot each other – my darling.'

She reached forwards then and took my head in her two hands. I was aware that her face was coming closer than it ever had before and for the first time our lips met. Then the squeal of the train's brakes sounded and she let go of my head. Incapable of movement, my whole being turned to vapour, or so it seemed. I was aware of her lifting her two cases, grunting slightly and then heaving them away towards the door. And a little later I heard the clank of carriages careering into each other and then the chuff-chuff of the engine as the train began to move out of the station. And only then did I find the power to act. With a cry of 'Fiona! Come back!' I leapt to my feet and dashed from the refreshment room – in time to see the rear of the train disappearing up the track.

I shall never know how I made my way back to the church hall. I have no memory of the trip. Wilson, who has been a brick in this matter, told me two days later that I entered like someone who had been to hell and returned. Apparently I stood limply for a moment in the doorway, eyes burning from an ashen face. Then, somehow finding the strength to do so, I straightened myself up and, patting my revolver, strode to my rightful place at the front of the platoon. I licked my parched lips and my eyes moved eloquently along the ranks of my men. And only then did I finally start to speak:

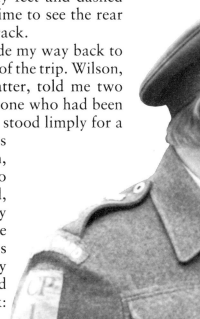

'Alright then, chaps, we've got a war to win. Put that lollipop away, Pike. Corporal Jones, you're facing the wrong way. Not now, Godfrey! Very well then: the correct use of the Mills bomb against enemy machine-gunners …'

IT WOULD SEEM almost impertinent to add anything to that powerful, and yet lyrical, account of what must have been one of the most formidable crises ever to occur in the personal life of an army commander. And yet there is one aspect – an aspect indeed not without its amusing side – which cannot be ignored. Captain Mainwaring, in his account of his doomed love for the beautiful Mrs Gray, remarks at one point: 'I'm absolutely sure that no one noticed anything untoward over the next few weeks. Sergeant Wilson, Corporal Jones, the humble rankers – to them I was the same dependable fearless officer that had always trained and led them. None of them suspected what turmoil was going on inside …'

I do not know if it would, in these circumstances, be seemly to state that we are 'fortunate' in having at our disposal documents which show clearly that the brave captain was quite wrong in his supposition. It is nevertheless the simple truth. For all his remarkable understanding of his men and his home community, Mainwaring does seem in those words to have fallen into a misconception that many brilliant and perceptive men have also held: the belief that their fellow townsfolk are far less aware than they themselves are of human suffering. The Mainwaring Dossier contains a rich supply of material demonstrating how mistaken Captain Mainwaring was in his belief that his desperate love for Mrs Gray had failed to make any impression on those around him.

The first document I have decided to print is notable not so much for its percipience as for its rarity. It is one of the very few communications in the entire Dossier in the hand of none other than the Captain's wife, Elizabeth Mainwaring. How this letter came into the possession of what, in the circumstances, we have to call the 'guilty party' can only be the subject of speculation. It may indeed, as in other similar cases, have been a discarded version that Mainwaring retrieved from a waste-paper basket in his home. Or possibly it was many years later than he came into possession of it. For our present purposes, the important consideration is that Mrs Mainwaring was not, as we know from many sources, a specially acute or indeed even very wide awake sort of woman, and yet it is clear from the relevant portions of this letter to her own mother that she was well aware of the nature of 'George's problem'. The letter is fairly long and I confine myself to printing the relevant section:

> *... two boxes of chocolates all to myself that time. Do you remember, mum? One was from that funny photographer that wanted me to pose on his stuffed camel and the other was from Aunt Maisie or someone. Even when he's got sweet coupons George hardly ever buys me chocolates any more. There's something a bit funny about George these days. In the shelter at nights I can hear him having dreams sometimes. He snuffles quite a lot and then says things like 'never', 'forever', 'how fair you are' – sounds just like a film. You remember the time that woman from the council kept chasing George? She was about sixty and had about ten warts on her face. George always came into the house running in case she was after him. This time it's different. Honestly, mum, I think he's doing the chasing this time. In his sleep I've also heard him say: 'love', 'kiss' and other stupid things like that. He groans and moans too. And he's distracted. Normally he says 'good morning' to me and 'goodbye' when he goes out – things like that. But just recently he doesn't even seem to notice me at all. I do hope the woman he's chasing has a good temper. Last thing we want is someone screaming around Walmington that George is chasing them. I wonder if he takes her chocolates? What I'd really like is one of those huge pre-war boxes of mixed hard and soft centres with little pictures of them so you know what all the centres are. Then you can just sit back in the armchair and ...*

But perhaps the most striking testimony to how unusual and conspicuous Captain Mainwaring's behaviour was at the time of his brief encounter with Mrs Gray is the fact that Frank Pike, forty-five years later in Australia, for once had a clear and not too garbled recollection of the episode.

No, I never knew her name. What's that you're sitting on? Oh goodness, it's one of my last three Kutey Koalas and you've ruined it. (Pause.) Really? Oh well, if you don't mind it being a little bent and crippled I don't mind giving you a good discount on it. For your little boy, is it? Oh, your old nanny? Well, I'm sure she'll love it. I'll give you five – no, six per cent discount – if I can work it out. What? Oh, him! He was always calling me 'stupid boy' but I reckon that he was a stupid man because all he did was moon about after that woman. Youcouldn't go anywhere without bumping into them: Ann's Pigsty or whatever it was called or if you went out into the countryside and sat down you'd see them sitting on a rock and holding hands. It was a terrible scandal. The whole of Walmington talked of nothing else for weeks. We all expected him to run off with her but then the bank would have sacked him, wouldn't it? And he'd have probably starved to death with her in the fields. Now I'll just wrap up this Kutey Koala and I'll throw in one of my Cheery Cockatoo Whistles which will please your old nanny no end, I'm sure. Would you consider being my agent in London and selling my super line of bush toys? Because if you would I could offer you . . .

It would not be difficult to fill pages with references to the Captain's romance from letters and journals penned in Walmington at the time. Corporal Jones, for example, in his terse notebook, has many entries concerning it. Here are just a sample: 'Saw Mainwaring with Gray woman again.' 'Mainwaring and Gray woman holding hands.' 'Mainwaring looking very gray because Gray woman gone.' And so on. Walker, in bawdy style, comments in a letter to a girl friend of his in the A T S:

Course I'm not having it away with anyone else. The only one in our platoon that's having any luck in that line is the guvnor. Old Mainwaring's got a nice bit of stuff from London. Very ladylike on the top but they're always the real goers underneath, right?' Ere, this'll kill you. Other day I saw Mainwaring and his lady nip behind a wall and guessing what for I sneaked up a bit and what did I hear? I heard a lot of snorting and blowing and naturally I thought: 'ello, he's going it some – at their age, they should be a bit more restrained like. Then I peeped over the wall and it was the 1:30 for London just steaming out of Walmington station. Nah, but seriously, he's making a right Charley of hisself and the whole town's pissing itself . . .

But in spite of the ribald and not very flattering views I have so far mentioned, and notwithstanding even Frazer's reference to 'a daft auld fool who's on the right course to wreck his body and ruin his reputation', it is pleasant to report that the great majority of the references I have found reveal affection and sympathy for the love-struck captain.

Prying eyes and gossip were ever the banes of small communities but Captain Mainwaring was held in such high esteem by his fellow citizens, and especially by the men who served under him, that the following affectionate reference is absolutely characteristic of the response to his one lapse from the paths of rectitude. It is, somewhat surprisingly, contained in a letter from Amy Samways whom, you will recall, was a friend of young Frank Pike. Although Miss Samways is several times referred to as having such a faint

voice as to be, for all intents and purposes, inaudible, the following passage –
written to her father, a chief petty officer in the navy – shows that the young
lady was capable of expressing herself very richly and poetically when she
chose. Once again we can only speculate as to how, or when, this document
came into Captain Mainwaring's possession.

> *... scarcely bear to see the suffering of poor Captain
> Mainwaring. This great-hearted and noble officer has
> contracted a most profound regard for a visitor to our fair
> town, an elegant and gracious young woman who rejoices in
> the name of Fiona Gray, such a romantic name, would you not
> agree, papa? Daily, I observe the distress of this couple,
> compelled by convention to mask their passion under the
> disguise of mere passing friendship. But the unmistakeable
> depth of their mutual yearning is betrayed by glances of such
> supernal brightness that ...*

Perhaps in compensation for her brief and inaudible spoken remarks Miss
Samway was a prodigious correspondent and the letter her father received
from her on this occasion, while serving on board a minesweeper in the North
Sea, consisted of no fewer than fifty-four closely packed pages. Too much to
print, I fear, but her tender sympathy expresses what many in Walmington
felt.

AND NOW IT is time to introduce the last entry from the immense log that we have space to include in this introductory volume. Some readers may be surprised by my choice. The episode does not show Mainwaring, or his platoon, in anything that could be described as a patriotic or a heroic light. There is a distinct element of rowdiness and disorder about the events it describes. It has no special military interest and does not mark a significant milestone in Mainwaring's career. Why then have I selected it as the last episode from Mainwaring's titanic log to include in this anniversary volume?

There is no single answer. It is partly, perhaps, because there is an element of 'happy ending' about it. Now it is true that the war still needed several years of hard campaigning before it was finally won. But in the episode that follows, while victory has by no means been achieved, it has become visible. A corner has been turned. It is no longer in doubt that the war will be won. And this spirit gives a kind of madcap zest to the episode. This is complemented by its subject, which concerns not hostility to a foe but hospitality to a friend – hospitality, however, that takes something of a disastrous turn.

Another reason for selecting this passage is that it tends to counter a criticism which I can imagine some readers making when my little book is published. It is conceivable that there are those who will find in the splendid Commander of the Walmington-on-Sea Home Guard platoon a rather plodding chap. They will say that he was brave, certainly, conscientious undoubtedly, patriotic beyond any question, but that despite these qualities he was little more than a dull-witted bank manager strutting about in uniform. It will be hard for such criticism to be levelled by those who have read this concluding section. The nimble and dextrous way with which, in the concluding pages, Mainwaring achieves his 'revenge' on the one who has wronged him clearly reveals not only an opportunist capable of creatively exploiting a fleeting chance, but a brilliant strategist. What such a man might have done had he been made a divisional or an army commander in the final assault on the German heartlands can only be left to amazed speculation.

14 JUNE 1942

I'VE LEARNED SOMETHING important in the past week. You won't find it in any of the training manuals. But for all that it's a very valuable lesson. It can be easier to fight the enemy than to remain at peace with your ally. At least with the enemy you know where you are. There's no divided interest. You just biff them and biff them and biff them. Until they surrender. Well, of course, they're not about to do that just yet. But as I told the men on parade a couple of weeks ago, we can begin to see the light at the end of the tunnel. I said to them:

'It's a long tunnel, and a very small light, but it's shining brightly for all to see.'

Private Pike commented: 'Mr Hodges won't like that, sir.'

The stupid boy had taken me literally. I had to explain that it was just a manner of speaking. I was talking about the war and the fact that it was now clear that the Hun was doomed. It might take a year. It might take several years but we now had the initiative. We were heading straight for Berlin and when we got there we'd kick Hitler in the seat of his pants. And the reason for my new optimism? It was because the Americans had come into the war. I'd have backed us all on our own. I'd have given seven to five to anyone that we'd make it in the long run. But it could have been a very hard slog indeed and at the end of it poor old England might have been looking a bit battered. But now, with all the dollars and the factories of the Yanks to help us crush Jerry, victory in the not-too-distant future was a certainty. I said cheerfully to the men:

'As you know the Americans came into the war a few months ago. Well, I'm happy to tell you that the first consignment of American soldiers is on its way over here from the USA.'

'Paddling over in canoes, are they?' asked Walker, in a sneering tone of voice.

'What's that supposed to mean?' I asked.

'Well, it's taken them two and a half years to get here.'

'None of that sort of talk,' I rebuked him, although I confess I felt a certain degree of sympathy with his remark.

Daily Mail
NO. 14.274 ONE PENNY * * * FOR KING AND EMPIRE
TUESDAY, JANUARY 27, 1942

LATE WAR NEWS SPECIAL

The first full and connected story of the smashing blow delivered by Allied naval and air forces against a great Japanese convoy in the Straits of Macassar is told by the Daily Mail New York correspondent below. This is the heaviest "knock" the Japanese have yet received, and there are indicatons that action continues.

JAPS DROWNED BY THOUSANDS

Troop-Fleet Meets Disaster

From DON IDDON NEW YORK, Monday.

FIRST full story of the amazing four-days-and-nights battle between Allied air and naval forces and a huge Japanese convoy trapped in the Macassar Straits, between Borneo and Celebes, is being told here to-night.

And even as the news-flashes reach New York an entire Japanese Expeditionary Force, aboard scores of large transports and escorted by numerous warships, ambushed and trapped in the Straits, is having the very life pounded out of it.

Flying Fortresses and other types of giant American and Dutch bombers are working in perfect co-ordination with United States destroyers and swift mosquito craft.

The R.A.F. is also believed to be taking part in the action.

The Japanese Fleet is ...eady in tatters, and an officially puts enemy losses ...1 troopships or warships, ...uding cruisers and de...yers sunk, and a further ...hips damaged.

...tish, Americans, and Dutch ...aging a sea-and-air battle of ...ilation, determined to send ... Japanese craft to the ...n.

... enemy death roll is already ...ed to be more than 15,000 ... This tremendous action has ...oing on since Friday, and will ...e until the whole Japanese ...ionary fleet has been wiped ...

...eat Cut off

...ts of the battle have come ...ay in a series of brief com...s. Only to-day was it ... that the united nations, ...he supreme command of Sir Archibald Wavell, had ...ly blocked all retreat to the enemy troop fleet, and was ...cally cutting it to pieces.

...cial statement said: "The ...icted on the Japanese con... the heaviest which the ...s suffered in any single since the war began."

... the course of the battle ...ologically:

Dutch heavy bombers, ...ombers, and fighters ... on a strong force of ... warships and transports, ... a dozen direct, crippling ...eight enemy ships. The ...ates destroyers followed ... a smashing night attack, ...h torpedoes and guns, ...ng numerous hits.

...enemy ship was blown ...e water, another was ... a third left listing ...

... Dutch and United ...ny bombers returned to ... with notable success. ... credited with two ...kings, severe damage ...re enemy vessels, and ... hit on a Japanese ...

...nited States cruisers ...ers again hammer the ...sion fleet, sending five ...ese transport to the ... claiming the probable ... sixth.

... War Department ...wing report: "Seven ...ng Fortresses took ...ack of January 24... ...anese convoy in the ...s, sinking one enemy ... setting fire to an...

...ion of Japanese ...ed the American ...were shot down and ...s returned to their ...d."

...ary feature of the ...was that the Ameri... ...presumably. British ... only negligible ...

...d Nations' warship ...amaged, and that ...e were no reports ...ugh it is certain ...een some.

...n of the great ...et when the jaws ...on it was probably ...neo, to reinforce ...o had already ... may have been ...th-east tip of the ... landings.

...server here sug...t have been in...ontal assault on ... it was bound, it ...

...acassar to-night ...he wreckage of ...ndreds of bodies ...o on the shores ...es.

...apanese were ...

[→] EIGHT

...the ...where American and Dutch sea and air forces smashed a Jap convoy.

SOVIET DRIVE TO THE WEST

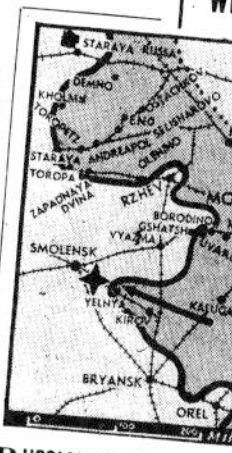

RUSSIAN forces are now approaching Smolensk in their drive westwards. The Germans themselves have admitted that their line has been pierced in the Yelnia region, only 50 miles south-east of Smolensk.—**See BACK Page.**

Ogilvie Quits BBC, Two Take Over

MR. F. W. OGILVIE, B.B.C. Director-General, has resigned, and for the rest of the war two men are to share the job.

Appointed to take over the post are:

Sir Cecil Graves, hitherto Deputy Director-General; and

Mr. Robert Foot, at present general adviser on war-time organisation to the governors.

Sir Cecil Graves. Mr. Robert Foot.

The B.B.C. announcement of this last night said: "In order to facilitate the reorganisation of the Corporation, which the Board of Governors has undertaken to meet existing conditions, the Director-General has placed his resignation in the hands of the Governors, and they have accepted it.

"The duties hitherto discharged by the Director-General will be entrusted for the duration of the war to two Directors-General jointly."

Reith's Successor

Mr. F. W. Ogilvie was appointed Director-General of the B.B.C. in succession to Sir John Reith in July 1938. He was formerly President and Vice-Chancellor of Queen's University, Belfast at £1,500 a year. At the B.B.C. his salary was £7,500 a year.

Sir Cecil George Graves, educated at Gresham's School, Holt, and Sandhurst, joined the B.B.C. in 1926; became Assistant Director of Programmes, first Director of the Empire service, Controller of Programmes, and then Deputy Director-General.

Mr. Robert William Foot, a solicitor, educated at Winchester; joined the Gas Light and Coke Company in 1919 and became general manager ten years later.

As chairman of the National Gas and Electricity Committee and of the London Regional Gas Centre, he helped with war problems in the metropolitan area.

£4,430,000,000 for U.S. Navy

From Daily Mail Correspondent

WASHINGTON, Monday. — The House of Representatives to-day rushed through the largest single naval appropriation in American history—£4,430,000,000—to speed the construction of America's "two-ocean Navy." It includes £2,000,000,000 for new warships.

Naval spending is contemplated at the rate of £250,000,000 a month.

RAF Day Raid on France

A patrol of R.A.F. fighters attacked several objectives, including a railway station, in Northern France yesterday afternoon. Two fighters are missing from other patrols.

Squadrons of bombers attacked the docks at Brest on Sunday night and all returned safely.

Another U.S. Ship Sunk

WASHINGTON, Monday. — The Navy Department announced to-day that the American-owned cargo-boat Venore, 8,016 tons, sank after two torpedo attacks off the Atlantic coast early on Saturday. Twenty-one survivors have been landed: 22 are still missing.—*Exchange.*

HEAVY JAP PRESSURE IN MALAYA

From Daily Mail Correspondent

SINGAPORE, Monday.

JAPANESE troops have once more succeeded by weight of numbers in driving back our left flank in Malaya. Batu Pahat has fallen after severe fighting.

The sighting of an enemy convoy off the port of Endau, which was evacuated some days ago, suggests that increasing pressure is also about to be brought to bear on our eastern flank.

In the centre, Kluang, where the railway to the north crosses the main lateral road in Southern Johore, is apparently still in British hands.

The whole of the Kluang area has been thoroughly "scorched," so that our retreat has not yet come to an end.

Sikh troops have inflicted some 500 casualties, with little loss to themselves, in the Kluang area in the past two days.

Axis radio stations to-night reported a "ferocious air battle over Kluang." This may well be true, but no details of any such action are available here.

Another Axis claim is that Japanese troops have landed on the west coast, nine miles south of Batu Pahat, so that new attempts at infiltration may have already begun.

U.S. RATIONS SUGAR

From Daily Mail Correspondent

New York, Monday.

SUGAR rationing, about 1lb. per week, will begin in the United States next month, it was officially announced to-day.

Canada, too, is to ration sugar immediately. The amount will be ¾lb. per week. No coupons or stamps will be used.

In the United States people who have hoarded sugar will be forced to give up excess supplies.

Girton Appoints New Head

Miss K. T. Butler, for 27 years a lecturer in modern languages at Girton College, Cambridge, has been appointed its head, from July 1. She succeeds Miss H. M. Wodehouse, who is retiring.

Miss Butler told *The Daily Mail* yesterday: "It is difficult to imagine quite what my job will be. At the moment we have 200 students, but the Government are considering whether our students are to be allowed to complete their three-years- course, or whether they must leave when they reach conscription age."

HIS HITLER MEDAL

The first foreign soldier to receive the Knight's Cross of the Iron Cross in this war is the Rumanian General Laccar, commander of ... Mountaineer ...

'THE YANKS' ARRIVE —FIGHTING FIT

Churchill Surprise

Broadcast Off: Heavy Cold

THE following official statement was issued last night:

"On medical advice, as he has not yet completely recovered from a heavy cold, the Prime Minister will not broadcast to-morrow evening, following upon the statement which he hopes to make in the House of Commons.

"Mr. Churchill hopes to broadcast at an early date."

AUSTRALIA WAITS

From RICHARD GREENLEES, Daily Mail Special Correspondent

MELBOURNE, Monday.

TENSION here about the help that Australia may expect from Britain now that invasion threatens these shores continues high.

Mr. Curtin's broadcast to-day, in which he said "No single nation can afford to risk its future on the infallibility of one man," is interpreted as a direct warning to Mr. Churchill that Australia will not be satisfied with half-measures.

The Federal Ministry yesterday indicated that it expected an early reply from Mr. Churchill on the Empire War Council proposal, but whether this offer will be acceptable is still doubtful.

London Minister

Non-Labour members of the Australian War Council are fully behind the Government members. Yesterday they endorsed the Government's steps to get supplies of aircraft and also approved of the principle of Australian representation on the Empire's Pacific War Councils.

It is suggested that Sir Earle Page, now in London on a Government mission, may be recalled if Britain is persuaded to agree to an Empire Council.

In that case, Dr. Evatt, Minister of External Affairs, is expected to be sent to London as resident Minister and the Australian member.

The Australian Press continues to emphasise that there is no selfish motive about Australia's demands for assistance in the Pacific theatre.

It is insisted that Australia is not claiming immunity from the dangers that other countries are facing. It is her view that wider demands of strategy render it essential that Japan must be prevented from capturing the main points of the northern archipelagos.

MILE LIMIT ON SHOP PARCELS

Retail shops are to restrict their deliveries to a radius of one mile from their shops and deliver only once a week. Under the pooling scheme they will deliver for one another, as part of the drive to save tyres, petrol, and labour.

Local traders' associations are working out details, and the complete scheme will be in operation by February 21.

Exceptions may be made in the case of stores who usually deliver in outlying districts and in rural areas where the mile limit would prevent traders from carrying out their normal business.

DESERT THREAT

ROMMEL is advancing north-eastward across Cyrenaica from Agedabia. Fighting is now taking place over a large area round Msus.

An Invasion Force

From Daily Mail Special Correspondent. BELFAST, Monday.

THE vanguard of the great American Expeditionary Force promised to Britain by President Roosevelt has arrived. The troops, commanded by Major-General Russell P. Hartle, were landed at a port in Northern Ireland. They were welcomed by Sir Archibald Sinclair, the Air Minister, the Duke of Abercorn, Governor of Northern Ireland, and British and American Army and Navy officials.

Sir Archibald Sinclair said to them: "Here perhaps you will join with us in withstanding the assault of our common enemy on this island fortress."

Then he made this significant statement: "From here assuredly you will sally forth with us to carry the war into his territory, and to free the oppressed peoples of Europe.

"Your safe arrival here marks a new stage in the World War.

"It is not an isolated manœuvre of war but part of the general disposition of our resources which is being made under the supreme responsibility of your President and our Prime Minister."

This is the first American force to reach the British Isles since war began except for groups of technicians and Staff officers.

Major-General Hartle is 52.

His 31 years' Army service includes duty in France in the 1914-18 war and in the Philippines and Puerto Rico.

He said to me, after I had

BACK PAGE—Col. FIVE

Rommel Overruns British Dumps

From ALEXANDER CLIFFORD, Daily Mail Special Correspondent CAIRO, Monday.

THE situation in Cyrenaica is serious. Rommel's thrusts have gone farther and quicker than even he could have expected. We have held him once or twice in a determined rear-guard action, but now he is more than 160 miles from his base.

He is operating across main tracks linking Benghazi with Mekili, and to-day's official communiqué puts the fighting north and north-east of Msus, the old Turkish capital guarding the important junction of desert tracks.

Msus is just 75 miles south-east from Benghazi. This means that Rommel has already outflanked most of the main road south of Benghazi.

It means that he has pushed aside our defensive screen, overrun all our forward dumps, and is threatening our communications south from the Green mountains.

There is no point in trying to sugar this pill—once again Rommel is looking very dangerous.

The main emphasis to-day here is placed on confusion in the fighting.

Shapeless Battles

It is the old story of shapeless battles in featureless scrub-covered desert, where nothing but exact figures can give any idea who is winning.

Unfortunately, in the fighting during the past few days we have been withdrawing from each battlefield. Our figures are likely therefore to be less exact than those of the enemy, who can count wreckage at their leisure.

It is no secret now that we were establishing dumps of petrol, ammunition, and supplies in forward areas with a view to future operations.

Already Rommel has run past most of these. We have, undoubtedly, been able to destroy a great many of them in time. Some we have been able to move.

But the speed of operations makes it virtually certain that some Nazi transport is now running on British petrol and some Axis troops eating British rations.

Petrol is the Army's lifeblood in these regions.

Hundreds of thousands of gallons are necessary both for advancing and retreating. It is to be hoped that our troops got all they need and that they have denied as much as possible to the Germans.

Vital Region

With each campaign it is clearer that the vital region of Cyrenaica is not the coast, but the desert inland.

Agedabia, Msus, Mekili are the important places, not Derna, Barce, and Benghazi.

And it is along this inner line, where there is not a drop of water or anything growing, that this present issue will be fought out.

Rommel's move is one of amazing daring. He has desperately left his safe defence line and come out to do battle in the open with a force whose size he cannot have known exactly.

It was a gambling risk such as Rommel appears to like, for he did the same thing when he broke through from Sidi Rezegh in November and drove back to the Egyptian border.

That time it failed. This time it may fail too, but he has got away to a good start.

Still it does not seem likely he can get right through to the Egyptian frontier again, assuming we go all out to stop him.

No Easy Way

But it appears now he will go on as far as his first swift momentum will carry him.

Things certainly are not critical yet.

Rommel still has 250 miles to go before he recovers what he lost.

There are plenty of defensive positions he will have to take before he gets through.

Our route for reinforcements is shorter and less vulnerable than his, and things are going to get harder for him as he proceeds, not easier ...

More Supply Ships Lost to Rommel

NEW and heavy toll is being taken of Axis convoys racing across the Mediterranean with men and tanks for Rommel's Africa Corps.

Following the all-day harrowing of the big convoy over the week-end came the news last night that two large and fully laden enemy tankers had been successfully attacked by submarines of the Mediterranean Fleet. It is considered that both were destroyed.

One was hit by three torpedoes and the other, which had both air and surface escort, was hit with two torpedoes.

An escorted convoy of three medium-sized transports has also been attacked and torpedo hits obtained on two of the vessels. One was seen to sink.

The Italian salvage vessel, Rampino has, in addition, been torpedoed and sunk by one of our submarines.

P.M. TO REVIEW TAX GRIEVANCE

War workers' income tax grievances are to be reviewed by Mr. Churchill, Colonel C. J. Hirst, president of Glasgow Chamber of Commerce, stated yesterday.

He said that Sir Ronald Matthews, president of the Association of British Chambers of Commerce, had been in direct touch with the Premier on the subject.

Mr. Churchill had asked for additional information, and chambers of commerce were now collecting it.

ICY GALE IN STRAIT

Strait weather last night: Freezing, with bitter north wind reaching gale force at times.

Hurricanes Attack Rangoon Raiders

From Daily Mail Correspondent RANGOON, Monday.

HURRICANES and Tomahawks went into action against Japanese fighters which attempted a sweep over the Rangoon area to-day. Three raiders are understood to have been shot down, two others probably destroyed, and a sixth damaged. The American Volunteer Group lost one Tomahawk.

Total enemy losses over Burma or on Japanese bases in Thailand are now 90 machines. Most of them have been destroyed in the past few days.

During the first days of the Pacific war the air defence of Burma was mainly in the hands of the older Brewster Buffalo fighters.

Another attack on Bangkok, the Thailand capital, is announced by R.A.F. headquarters here. This time the docks and commercial area were bombed, and big fires started.

One of our aircraft failed to return.

To-day's army communiqué reports that there was no change on the Tenasserim (Moulmein) front.

A British officer and 100 Gurkhas who were cut off some days ago and believed lost have fought their way back to our lines.

It is announced to-day that General Wavell recently paid a flying visit to Rangoon in an American Army plane.

Some observers believe that ... Chinese ...

DUCE CUTS WAR INDUSTRIES

BERNE, Monday.—The whole of Italy's industry has been reduced to a five-days week because of the shortage of electric power.

A report to the *Neue Zuercher Zeitung* (the Swiss newspaper) said that the low-water level in the country's reservoirs had forced a 20 per cent. reduction of current to all factories.

This had been met by closing the factories for another day each week in addition to Sunday.—*A.P.*

Pearl Harbour Blame

From Daily Mail Correspondent

WASHINGTON, Monday.—The White House to-day indicated that further action concerning Admiral Kimmel and Lieut.-General Short, the United States Commanders at Hawaii at the time of ...

'FINUCANE' SQUADRON

By COLIN BEDNALL, Daily Mail Air Correspondent

Flight-Lieut. "Paddy" Finucane, 21-years-old D.S.O. and triple D.F.C., killer of 24 enemy aircraft, has been promoted Squadron Leader, and will command the famous 602 Spitfire squadron.

Another ace, Flight-Lieut. Keith Truscott, D.F.C., has also been promoted Squadron Leader. He will lead the Australian Spitfire squadron No. 452, with which Finucane scored many successes.

An Australian, Truscott is the first man trained under the Empire scheme to reach squadron leader's rank.

Squadron Leader Finucane has flown and fought in the squadron which he is now to lead, a unit which distinguished itself in the Battle of Britain.

Halifax Sees U.S. Treasury Chief

WASHINGTON, Monday. — Lord Halifax conferred to-day with Mr. Henry Morgenthau, Secretary of the United States Treasury, but they declined to discuss the nature of the conference.—*A.P.*

FIRST DAY ALERT IN SAN FRANCISCO

San Francisco, Monday.—First daylight Alert, lasting four hours, sounded here as a result of unidentified planes, which disappeared before they could be identified.—B.U.P.

MORE S. AFRICAN POLICE GAOLED

Capetown, Monday. — Eight traffic constables and 29 members of prison staff have been detained at Johannesburg as part of the round-up of police accused of subversive activity.—Exchange.

After all, it was quite clear that the Yanks had only come into the war because the Japs had given them a pasting at Pearl Harbor. Oh, I know the Yanks had been very helpful to us, sending us a lot of dried eggs and old destroyers, but who'd had to bear the brunt of defending the free world? We had. And pretty much on our own. Still, the Americans were now coming and better late than never. Some of them, what's more, were coming to Walmington-on-Sea.

'When can we expect them, sir?' asked Frazer respectfully.

'A small advance guard will be arriving on Saturday morning. Now it's clear that we must give our brave allies a hearty welcome.'

'You mean,' drawled Wilson in his bored tone of voice, 'roll out the red carpet for them, sir?'

'Precisely. Well, naturally we haven't actually got a red carpet ...'

Walker immediately said: 'I could get you a roll of American cloth, sir.'

'No, I don't think –' I began but was interrupted by Corporal Jones.

'Permission to speak, sir?'

'Go ahead, Jones.'

'We must take our American cousins to our bosoms and nurture them. We must take them into our homes,' he said excitedly.

'Exactly, Jones,' I agreed.

Pike said in a sullen tone of voice, 'Well, I don't think my mum would like to have a lot of strange Americans in the house.'

'In time of war, Pike,' I explained to the rather unintelligent youth, 'one cannot afford to choose one's bedfellows.'

'I don't think my mum would like having them for bedfellows either,' insisted Pike. 'Nor would Uncle Arthur – that is Sergeant Wilson – would you, Uncle Arthur?'

'There's no question of that, Frank,' said Wilson, clearly somewhat embarrassed.

'Alright, let's get on,' I said impatiently. 'Are there any other suggestions for welcoming our new allies?'

NOT A STAB IN THE BACK PERHAPS, BUT CERTAINLY A BLOW IN THE NECK. WHILE NO HARD EVIDENCE OF TREACHERY HAS COME TO LIGHT, THE NUMEROUS EXAMPLES OF OBSTRUCTIONISM THAT MAIN-WARING ADDUCES IN HIS GREAT LOG DO MAKE ONE WONDER IF WARDEN HODGES MIGHT NOT HAVE BEEN 'ACTING UNDER SPECIFIC INSTRUCTIONS FROM THE REEKS CHANCELLERY'.

IN AN ENVELOPE INSCRIBED, IN CAPTAIN
MAINWARING'S HANDWRITING, 'IDEAS
FOR WELCOMING AMERICANS', I FOUND
THE FOLLOWING INTRIGUING PHOTO-
GRAPHS.

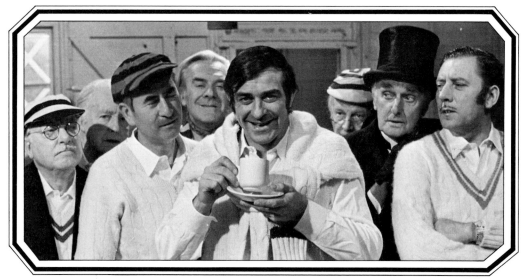

BEARING HARDSHIP WITH A SMILE: THE PLATOON CRICKET TEAM IN THE PAVILION DURING TEA BREAK. NOTE HOW, DURING THIS PERIOD OF ACUTE WARTIME SHORTAGES, THE TEAM EAGERLY AWAIT THEIR TURN FOR A SIP.

'Mr Mainwaring, sir,' exclaimed Jones. 'I have just been struck by a thought. When I was in the Sudan, and we signed a peace treaty with the Fuzzy-Wuzzies, General Kitchener thought it would be a good idea to have a get together. So we asked those bloodcurdling savages what they'd like to do, and they said they wanted a spear-throwing competition. At first we thought this was quite a good idea but a problem soon came up.'

'What was that?' I asked.

'They wanted to use General Kitchener as the target. But in the end we managed to talk them out of it and all of us British soldiers lined up to throw our spears. Well, the Fuzzy-Wuzzies was standing right behind us with their spears waiting for their turn to throw. So when my turn came I stepped back to get more force to my throw —'

Impatient with Jones's long, rambling account, I said sharply:

'Get to the point, Jones.'

'That's just what I did, sir,' exclaimed the indignant corporal. 'I got the Fuzzy-Wuzzy's spear up me — not all the way up but —'

'Yes, yes, we understand, Jones,' I silenced him hastily.

'Anyway, what I was trying to say, sir, is that we could do something along the same lines for the Yanks and invite them to watch a darts match at the Red Lion.'

I blinked at Jones in astonishment. It was, as far as I could recollect, the only sensible suggestion he'd made since his idea for stopping the runaway secret weapon by hanging upside down from a railway bridge and snipping off its antenna.

'Excellent, Jones, excellent,' I complimented him. 'An evening in a typical English pub. What could be better? The whole platoon will be present and you can all bring your ladies.'

'I'll bring Shirley, sir,' said Walker with a grin. 'You know what she's like.'

I shuddered faintly at the recollection of the brassy young lady he had referred to. I had last seen her doing a strange, immodest dance called, I believe, a jitterbug, at the golf club's annual binge the year before.

I contented myself with nodding.

'And I'll bring my girl,' lisped Pike. 'That's Amy. She doesn't say much but she's nice. And Uncle Arth – I mean Sergeant Wilson will bring my mum, won't you, Uncle Sergeant?'

'Yes, yes, very likely, Frank,' said Wilson hurriedly. He turned to me. 'Will you bring your wife, sir?' he asked.

It was on the tip of my tongue to say 'yes'. I had had, just for a moment, an image of a lady a bit like Elizabeth but somehow with more – more sociable qualities – being a gracious hostess. But then the reality chased this picture from my mind. I shook my head.

'No, I don't think so, Wilson. Somehow I can't see Elizabeth doing

JONES, WITH HIS CELEBRATED CRY OF, 'THEY DON'T LIKE IT UP 'EM', DEMONSTRATES HOW HE WOULD DEAL WITH GERMAN SPIES APPROACHING OUR SHORES USING UNDERWATER BREATHING EQUIPMENT.

Keep mum
she's not so dumb!

CARELESS TALK COSTS LIVES

NOT THE LEAST OF WARTIME HARDSHIPS WAS THE NEED FOR SOLDIERS TO CENSOR
EVERYTHING THEY SAID FOR FEAR OF INADVERTENTLY CONVEYING INFORMATION TO
THE ENEMY. THE SENIOR OFFICERS CLUSTERED ROUND THE 'MATA HARI' FIGURE ABOVE
WOULD HAVE BEEN WELL AWARE OF THIS DANGER. BUT EVEN CORPORAL JONES, IN HIS
HOMELY CONVERSATIONS WITH MRS FOX, WOULD HAVE HAD TO REMIND HIMSELF THAT
SHE COULD HARDLY BE QUITE AS 'DUMB' AS SHE SOMETIMES SEEMED.

very much for Anglo-American relations.'

'I have an idea, sirr,' exclaimed Frazer eagerly, rolling his eyes in his enthusiasm and speaking with such a pronounced highland burr that I could hardly comprehend him. 'Why don't we have a banner stretched along the bar, with a message of greeting on it? Something like: "Intae battle together, boys, and wade through the gore of the slaughtered foe".'

'With a skull at each end?' suggested Walker, grinning.

'That's enough, Walker,' I said, suppressing a smile. 'The banner's an excellent idea, Frazer, but the message will have to be simpler and more hospitable. Something like: "Welcome to our Brave Allies".'

'Would you like my sister Dolly to make it, sir?' asked Godfrey in his slightly quavery, but also courteous, voice. 'She does very fine embroidery.'

'Could she do it in the time?' I asked doubtfully.

Godfrey looked thoughtful for a moment and then shook his head. 'Probably not, sir, no. The last time she did any embroidery it took her three months and that was only my name: Charles. On my towel actually. Of course it did have the most exquisite roses and curling vines embroidered round my name but they might not be appropriate for a military occasion.'

'Thank you, Godfrey,' I said patiently. 'I think I can arrange to have the banner printed down at the offices of the *Walmington Record*. Well then, men, I think we've cracked it. The Americans may have given up being a colony a long time ago, but that's no reason why we shouldn't give them a royal welcome, is it?'

◆ 〈 〈 ◆ 〉 〉 ◆

The evening arrived and I duly proceeded to the bar. Quite a few of the others were there already. I noticed that the women all looked very smart, much smarter in fact that I ever recalled seeing them. Mrs Fox, who often accompanies Corporal Jones, was wearing a kind of outfit that certainly made the most of her bosom as anyone could see, and no one could deny that Mrs Fox is well equipped in the bosom line. I personally felt that perhaps a little more dress and less bosom might have been more satisfactory but there you are. Mrs Pike, who was sitting between her son Frank and Sergeant Wilson, was looking very trim in a new dress that must have used up her clothing coupons for the whole year I should imagine. Even Pike's girl, called Amy I seem to recall and a girl with such a faint voice that only young Pike has ever been able to make out what she's saying, was very smart. I didn't see Walker's girl and assumed, quite correctly, that she hadn't arrived yet.

The banner was there, draped above the bar and looking very hospitable. It didn't say 'Welcome to our Brave Allies', as I had originally intended, because that much lettering had proved prohibitively expensive. Instead, it proclaimed with simple warmth: 'Welcome Buddies'. I hadn't actually been acquainted with the term 'Buddy' before, but Wilson assured me that it was the normal American word signifying friendship. He explained that if two cowboys happened to meet on some trail in the wild west one of them would probably say: 'Good day, buddy.' Then the other would be likely to reply: 'Good day to you, buddy, and would you care for a spot of chewing tobacco?' Of course we didn't have any chewing tobacco but we did have cigarettes and pipe tobacco and we were determined than the Americans should not pay for a thing that evening. They were to be our guests and all money for drinks was to come from platoon funds.

The vicar was present and consuming a drink that looked like scotch and soda. I was pleased to see this since the vicar had got up the opposing team and I was keen that we would beat them. I knew that the vicar had a slight weakness for whisky and that he tended very quickly to get unsteady on his feet when he drank it. Obviously the more unsteady he got the better our chances of winning the darts tournament and impressing our new American bud – er – friends.

Altogether there was that feeling of cosiness and good-fellowship which is the characteristic atmosphere of the English pub and I felt sure the evening would be a successful one. I still cannot imagine how every conceivable thing managed to go wrong and we ended up with a total shambles.

'Hello,' said a female voice beside me.

I looked round and smiling at me in a rather brassy but still friendly way was Walker's current young lady, Shirley. She was the one I had once seen doing a dance called the jitterbug with Walker in the banqueting room of the White Hart. It was a very athletic dance, the chief purpose of which, as far as I could see, was to display the lingerie of the girls engaged in it. On the present occasion, Shirley was wearing rather a tight outfit which would have been quite unsuitable for jitterbuggering in but which nonetheless managed to look very sensual.

'Oh, good evening,' I replied, trying to keep a tone of disapproval from my voice.

But she seemed completely oblivious to criticism and asked cheerfully: 'Seen Joe?'

'Er, no – Walker doesn't appear to have arrived yet.'

'Like my outfit?'

'Yes, it's – er – very striking.'

'Not too tarty, is it? I was aiming for the demure look. Don't want these Yanks to get the wrong idea about us English girls, do we?'

I was spared the necessity of finding a tactful reply by the arrival of a man with a large Celtic nose and a big camera with a flashbulb prominently attached to it.

'Good evening, Captain Mainwaring,' he greeted me with that sing-song lilt of the Welsh that you don't hear very often on the Sussex coast.

'Good evening,' I replied with a pleasant smile.

'My name's Cheeseman. I'm from the *Eastbourne Gazette*. I'm hoping to take a few pictures of you greeting our American allies.'

Naturally this project met with my wholehearted approval. 'Excellent,' I enthused.

Cheeseman glanced at Shirley who was still stationed beside me and, with a faintly suggestive smile I felt, asked: 'This your good lady then?'

'My – oh no. No, she's with one of my platoon, a Private Walker.'

'And I think I'd better go and see what he's up to. Tarra,' said Shirley cheerfully, and minced away with a pronounced swinging motion of her hindquarters.

Cheeseman watched her in what was apparently appreciative silence for a moment or two and then turned to me again. 'I'm doing a series of articles for the *Gazette* entitled: "The Doughboy meets the Tommy". Brilliant idea, wouldn't you say? Your pub evening here is going to be the subject of the first article in the series.'

'I'm delighted,' I said. 'Just one thing. Could you give me some kind of signal when you're about to take a photograph?'

Cheeseman frowned in a puzzled kind of way. I explained:

'So that I can take off my spectacles. Gives me more of a soldierly appearance, I like to think.'

Cheeseman looked me up and down and shrugged slightly. 'If you say so, boyo,' he agreed.

Wilson appeared at my side. 'They seem to be a bit late, sir,' he suggested.

I glanced at my watch. 'A minute or two perhaps. I'm told, Wilson, that there will be some sort of colonel in charge of the Americans. Now you know about their lingo. How should I greet him?'

'Quite informally I should say, sir. He'll probably greet you with: "Howdy partner, put it there".'

I gave a faint snort of disbelief. 'Oh come on, Wilson, we're not on the cowboy trail now. This is a senior officer in the American forces. I think you and young Pike see too many American films.'

'I assure you, sir, he'll greet you with: "Howdy partner, put it there".'

I am not much of a gambling man but I was about to propose a small wager to Wilson about this preposterous suggestion when Hodges, in his A R P uniform complete with tin helmet, breezed up beside me.

'Evening, Napoleon,' he said impertinently, with his customary inane grin. 'What time's the match then? I can't wait for our team to take you Home Guards apart.'

'The darts match is scheduled for nine o'clock,' I informed him.

He frowned in apparent irritation. 'Why so late?'

'As I assumed you were aware, we're putting on this darts match for the benefit of our American visitors.'

Hodges gave a snort of contempt. 'Oh blimey,' he exclaimed. 'I hate the blooming Yanks. Loud-mouthed, overbearing lot. I just can't stand them.' With this he thumped the bar hard with his first and bawled at the barman who was attending to a customer some distance away, 'Hey! Let's have some service!'

Just then Walker hurried into the saloon bar and made his way towards me. 'They're here, Mr Mainwaring,' he said. 'Two jeep loads of them just pulling up as I arrived.'

'Thank you, Walker,' I said and turned to Corporal Jones. 'Corporal, get the men lined up.'

'Very good, sir,' said Jones, leaping to his feet from his place beside the ample Mrs Fox into whose ear he had been whispering something.

'Line up! At the double! Line up!' he bawled.

'Keep it informal,' I instructed him.

'Line up, keeping it informal, at the double!' he changed the command.

The men left their lady guests and formed a ragged line. I was astonished to see, in the line-up, Walker's young lady, Shirley, in her skin-tight outfit, teetering on very high heels, and the plump Mrs Fox.

'No, not you ladies,' said Corporal Jones.

'I don't want to be left out, you know,' said Mrs Fox huffily.

Shirley contributed: 'I'm sure the Yanks would rather meet us than all you old men.'

I saw it was necessary for me to take a hand. 'I'm afraid I shall have to insist that you sit down, ladies,' I informed them.

Grumbling audibly they went back to their tables. I heard Shirley saying bitterly to Mrs Fox: 'Blimey, don't tell me we've put on these glad rags for nothing.'

I glanced at Cheeseman. He had his camera at the ready. To be on the safe side I removed my glasses. I instructed Wilson: 'You can present me to the colonel and vice versa, Wilson.'

'Very well, sir,' he drawled in an amused kind of way.

At that very moment, the outside door opened and through it came a dark, thick-set officer who looked as if he might be Spanish or Turkish or something of that sort, followed by a sergeant and six privates, all dressed in the rather la-di-da, to my way of thinking, tailored uniforms of the American army. I saw Wilson approach the officer and then the two of them came towards me. As he got near enough to be heard above the noise of voices and the clink of glasses the officer stretched out his hand and, to my astonishment, said: 'Howdy partner. Put it there.'

For a moment I merely gaped at him. It even flashed through my mind that Wilson had put him up to it. But I rallied quickly and took his hand, saying: 'Howdy, buddy. Here it is.'

I noticed Wilson smirking behind him. I put my glasses back on and saw that his lips framed the words: 'I told you so.'

But then I, and I assume everyone else, was momentarily blinded by the brilliant flash from Cheeseman's camera as he recorded this, in a small way, historic scene.

'Now then, Colonel,' I said courteously. 'I want to welcome you and your men to Walmington-on-Sea and to express the hope that you have a very enjoyable evening with us. While you're our guests we want you to make yourselves completely at home and to do exactly what you want to do.'

To my surprise, the colonel then turned towards his detachment and roared: 'You heard the captain, boys. Go to it!'

At which, with a whoop suggestive of the Red Indians assailing General Custer on the occasion of his last stand, the Americans swarmed over to the tables where the ladies were sitting and, within moments, were showering them with gifts, many of which looked like intimate articles of clothing, and kissing them on their ears. My men gazed at this spectacle in open-mouthed amazement. Disdaining the fact that they were on licensed premises, the Americans also produced bottles of various potent drinks and began taking gulps straight from them while filling the ladies' glasses with the same. I was utterly flabbergasted. However, the colonel did not join in this unseemly riot but simply lit a big cigar and gazed benignly at his rabble.

My men were still lined up although showing a tendency towards restlessness. Indeed at one point Private Pike broke ranks and hurried over to his mother and I heard him say: 'Mum, that American's got his arm round Amy. Make him take it away, mum. Make him take it away!'

But Mrs Pike, who was herself flanked by two American soldiers, one of whom was waving a pair of gauzy stockings in front of her while the other was patting her knee, merely glanced at Pike with a distant look as if she barely recognised him. Naturally I had to summon him back to the ranks before there was a general insurrection. Then I embarked on the thankless task of presenting my men to the colonel.

'This is Lance-Corporal Jones,' I said, hoping that Jones would keep his welcome brief. It proved a vain hope.

'I'm pleased to meet you, sir,' began the veteran. 'I had the honour of serving with the Americans in France in 1917. They used to call us Limeys.

WALKER PREPARES TO SHOW THE YANKS HOW TO GET THREE BULLS WITH THREE DARTS. BUT THE GUESTS SEEM MORE INTERESTED IN WHAT CAN BE OBTAINED AT THE BAR – AND THAT DOESN'T NECESSARILY MEAN BOOZE!

Do you know why that was, sir?'

'I'm sure the colonel knows all about it, Jones,' I intervened.

'Not at all,' protested Schultz, as I had learned the colonel was named.

'Well, sir,' began Jones. 'In times of old on British ships, the sailors used to get all scurvy and mingy ...'

The tale seemed to go on forever and ended with Jones giving an imitation of a sailor being flogged. The colonel merely gaped at him throughout. When it was finally over I hurried the American on to the next man. But Frazer's approach was, if anything, even more embarrassing. He fixed the colonel fiercely with his rolling eye and boomed:

> 'How the day, and now's the hour.
> See the front o' battle lour,
> See approach proud Hitler's power ...'

"LET US GO FORWARD TOGETHER"

He went on to quote the whole of a long, incomprehensible poem that he claimed was by Robert Burns, with modern additions, such as the use of the name of Hitler, by himself. The colonel again gaped, clearly not understanding a word. Then Godfrey presented the colonel with a tin containing, he proclaimed, an upside-down cake baked by his sister, Dolly.

When we finally reached the end of the line, the Colonel turned to me and, nodding, said: 'You've certainly got some veterans in your outfit, Captain. I didn't know that the British Army took them so old.'

I was about to explain to the colonel the exact nature of the Home Guard when, to my surprise and dismay, I heard Wilson, who was just behind me, say:

'Well, of course, we're not real soldiers.'

I turned on him indignantly. 'What are you talking about, Wilson?' I rebuked him. 'Of course we're real soldiers.'

He smiled in a pained kind of way. 'But we're not, sir,' he held his ground. 'Not really. We're Home Guards.'

'And what exactly are Home Guards?' asked the colonel, puffing on his cigar.

'We're sort of part-time soldiers,' Wilson elaborated. 'You see, Mr Mainwaring's the bank manager. I'm his chief clerk and the others are shopkeepers and – that sort of thing. We were formed to protect the town against German parachute troops and so forth.'

Schultz smiled in a fatherly way. He actually patted Wilson's arm. 'Well, you guys don't have to worry any more. We'll do all the defending there is to do around here from now on. You old-timers can just relax and take things easy.'

Naturally, I was outraged by this patronising tone and began to say so. 'Now, look here, Colonel –'

But Wilson interrupted, saying pointedly, 'Don't you think it's time we gave the colonel a drink, sir?'

I realised that he was reminding me that this was meant to be an occasion of good-will and I choked back my resentment.

'Yes, of course.' I turned to the colonel. 'How would you like to try a glass of real English beer, sir?'

'Very much indeed,' said Schultz.

I accordingly went to the bar and purchased a pint of foaming bitter which I carried back to the colonel. As I handed it to him, I heard a kind of stage whisper from Cheeseman who was standing nearby: 'Captain Main-waring!'

I realised he was about to take a picture and I reached up and removed my glasses as the colonel lifted the pint pot to his lips. A moment later there was a blinding flash and a shower of rain. At least that's what it felt like. It was actually the colonel spewing out, with an expression of disgust, the large gulp of beer he had taken.

'What the hell is that? Horse pi- – er – warm dishwater?' he exclaimed angrily.

'It's best bitter, actually,' said Wilson in a faintly amused tone of voice.

'It's disgusting! Haven't you guys ever heard of ice?' asked the scowling officer.

I tried to save the situation. 'Is there anything else you'd care for, sir?' I asked.

He nodded. 'I'll have a Scotch on the rocks,' he said loudly.

The licensee caught this remark and called over. 'Sorry. No Scotch.'

The colonel shook his head reproachfully. 'What kind of hospitality is this, anyway?'

'The best we can manage,' murmured Wilson, a trifle tactlessly I felt.

'What's that supposed to mean?' asked the disgruntled colonel.

It was most unfortunate that it was precisely at this juncture that the loud-mouthed Hodges breezed up to us. He unceremoniously took the colonel's hand and shook it up and down vigorously, causing the colonel to spill some of the beer he was still holding down the front of his uniform. The colonel gazed at Hodges in astounded anger but it was wasted on the brash fellow.

'Hello, Colonel, my name's Hodges. I met your lot when they came out to France in 1917. Of course, we'd been expecting you.'

'Oh,' nodded the colonel, looking a little mollified. 'I see.'

'That's right,' continued Hodges with an insolent grin. 'We'd been expecting you for three years ever since the war started in 1914. Still you quickly polished off the enemy for us, didn't you? And now I suppose you've come to do the same again? Well, it's an improvement. It's only been two and a half years this time. Maybe if there's another war you'll make it before we've done all the really hard work on our own. But then you Yanks never did like fighting much, did you?'

'Maybe,' said the colonel in a rather low thoughtful voice that struck me as more reflective than angry. 'But we realise there are times when it's unavoidable.'

At just that moment the voice of Cheeseman sounded again. 'Captain Mainwaring!'

I reached up and removed my glasses and a split second later all the lights went out. Or so it seemed. I learned later that Hodges, seeing the colonel's fist approaching him at high velocity, had ducked and so my right cheek had become its recipient. I have to say that the American officer packed quite a punch. They told me afterwards that I was totally unconscious for nearly two minutes and after that I remained a trifle hazy about events. I had the impression that the whole bar-room had become full of thrashing, shouting soldiers, and this, I learned later, was pretty much what had really happened. It's ironic that the only hand-to-hand fighting the platoon ever did, after nearly three years of war, was against an ally rather than the enemy.

CHEESEMAN FROM THE *EASTBOURNE GAZETTE*, WHOSE UNLUCKY SNAP NEARLY GAVE THE GERMAN PROPAGANDA MACHINE A BONANZA.

I HAVE MADE IT a principle thus far to print the entries from Captain Mainwaring's gigantic log intact and without interruption. But I feel I should make an exception in the present case. The reason is, of course, that some of the most important events in the story took place while he was unconscious. This was only for a brief period admittedly but it was precisely then that the platoon flew into furious action. I cannot in all conscience exclude from this section of my book at least a brief selection of quotes from letters and diaries written by others present on that hectic occasion.

. . . always been hard to rouse to violence, as you know, Barney, but this wretched doughboy, with three upside-down stripes on his arm, was being disgustingly familiar with – well, a village woman, actually, by the name of Mavis – whom I've always kept a protective eye on. She has a son called Frank who's quite a – well a – quite tall young fellow really – and I like to help him along if I can because Mavis – the village woman – has been – well pretty decent to me in many ways. So when I asked the rotten doughboy sergeant to take his lecherous paws – which I think was the expression I used –

from around Mavis and he simply grinned at me and said something rude, I'm afraid I rather lost my temper. I tapped him once or twice on the head with a full bottle of bourbon whisky and I confess I felt a distinct sense of satisfaction at seeing him slide to the floor with his eyes glazing over. By this time all the chaps in the platoon were apparently engaged in some kind of strife with the doughboys and — well, I've done a little sketch of it from memory — not very good, I know, but it might give you some idea of the jolly proceedings. The venison pâté was quite delicious, Barney, and I assume you've had a good stalking season? Which moor did you . . .

(Letter from Sergeant Wilson to his
brother Sir Barnington Wilson of Danbigh, Yorks.)

Had this Yank in deadly Dervish death-grip. Just as banging his head on floor to finish him off Mrs Fox hit me with a bottle. Silly woman.

(An unusually long diary entry by L/Cpl Jones.)

. . . actually knocked the glass of whisky from my hand. Whisht, Angus, and is there a Scot breathing air that wouldnae revenge himself on such a wrong? But sensible of my standing as one of the senior members of the platoon and likely to be made CO when Mainwaring finally

becomes too corpulent to waddle along behind us, I merely gave him a little push. The mon was clearly drunk because he flew off the rostrum and continued on through the window sustaining severe cuts and other injuries ...

(Letter from Private Frazer to reclusive
ex-fisherman brother Angus in the Hebrides.)

... you know me, darling, one of nature's peacemakers. Trouble is the only way to make peace sometimes is with an iron bar. On this occasion I thought I'd try getting a sing-song going to turn everyone's thoughts from bloodshed. So I started singing and conducting at the same time. Trouble was I had a bottle in each hand and as I was conducting the bottles sometimes came into contact with the faces of some of the yanks ...

(Letter from Private Walker to a girl called
Ruby Lovebug at an address in Soho, London.)

... a most distressing scene, Maidie. Naturally I would never have become involved with anything so ungentlemanly. But when I saw this American using slices of Dolly's upside-down cake as missiles something inside me snapped. I was standing on the rostrum and so it was quite an easy matter

to take up one of the folding chairs and bring it down upon his head. He thereupon ceased throwing upside-down cakes and went to sleep and I decided it was high time to return to the cottage. Thank you so much for the dental floss, Maidie, which I shall try to remember to use, as you recommend, morning and night . . .

(Letter from Private Godfrey
to his sister, Maidie.)

I think that suffices to provide the reader with some idea of the 'flavour' of the occasion. We will now let Captain Mainwaring take up once more the thread of the narrative.

Well, there was the most colossal row about the fight. Nearly turned into an international incident. Cheeseman's picture showed Colonel Schultz's fist connecting with my left cheek. The picture was printed not only in the *Eastbourne Gazette* but in several national dailies too. The caption to it read simply: Captain 'Tommy Atkins' meets Colonel 'G.I. Joe'. I had this picture in one hand as I spoke to our divisional colonel on the telephone the following day.

'I assure you, sir,' I explained, 'that it was in no way our fault. Hodges made an insulting remark. The American went to hit him. Hodges ducked and I received the blow. My men were utterly innocent.'

'I accept that, Mainwaring,' said the crackly voice at the other end of the line, 'but the fact remains that a photograph of you, brawling with an American, is on the front page of just about every blessed British paper. The German propaganda machine will have a field day with it. I mean, how does it look? The Americans have only been in the country a few hours and they're

PUNCH-UP IN PUB

The old KO in Sussex. Hey there, colonel, he's on our side. That's Captain George Mainwaring of the Walmington-on-Sea Home Guard platoon you're laying into.

So what went wrong? Our chaps prepared a jolly evening in an English pub to welcome their GI friends and before you could say: 'put it there, buddy', fists and furniture were flying. Still, we're told it was all a misunderstanding and so the Germans had better not assume that together we're not going to batter them into submission. Because we jolly well are. Right, chaps? And, guys? You see, Colonel Shultz, we just don't drink ice-cold beer in our pubs and so ...

fighting with British troops. The thing's got to be nipped in the bud.'

'I understand, sir. But how?'

'I'm sending that reporter over to your HQ again. I want you to ask the American colonel round and make a public apology –'

'You mean crawl?' I asked indignantly.

'Yes, crawl if necessary, Mainwaring. This thing is too important for hurt pride. One of the penalties of wearing pips on your shoulder is that you sometimes have to carry the can for things which aren't your fault. See that it's done.'

'But, sir, I –'

But it was too late. The colonel had hung up. I sat for a moment in thought and then I stood up and looked into the small mirror on the shelf behind my desk. It showed a large, angry, purple bruise on my cheek. While I was thus engaged the door to my office opened and Wilson entered.

'Oh dear!' he exclaimed, in a rather theatrical manner I felt. 'You do look a sight!'

'Well, so would you if you'd had the colonel's fist to contend with. Consider yourself lucky, Wilson.'

'Oh, I do, sir.'

'The worst of it is – the picture's in all the papers. All the bank's customers will really believe that I've been brawling.'

'Oh I'm sure they'll give you the benefit of the doubt, sir. Actually I came out rather well in the picture, didn't you think? Do you suppose the paper would let me have some prints if I wrote to them?'

'For your many fans, Wilson?' I asked with cutting irony.

'Exactly, sir,' he replied, impervious as always to any hint of criticism. 'Whatever made you antagonise Schultz the way you did, sir?'

I gazed at Wilson indignantly for a moment but then something about what he'd said struck me.

'Just a minute, Wilson,' I said, 'Schultz is a German name, isn't it?'

'That's right, sir.'

'Well, what's a German doing in the American army?'

'There are quite a lot of people with German names in America, sir. Most Americans came from somewhere in Europe originally.'

'Well, I think the whole thing's getting out of hand – people with German names fighting on our side. It was much better when we were on our own.

At least we all knew who was who and what was what.'

'Possibly, sir, but –'

Just then there was a knock at the outer door to my office and I called: 'Come in.'

To my considerable surprise none other than Colonel Schultz, accompanied by his sergeant, entered. Schultz immediately put out his hand and smiled. 'I've come to offer my heartfelt apologies,' he said.

'Oh, it's quite alright,' I said, a trifle stiffly perhaps.

'But it's not,' insisted Schultz. 'You and your men had laid on that fine entertainment for us and I allowed myself to be nettled by that – that – what was he, anyhow?'

'Hm? Hodges? Oh, he's the A R P warden – civil defence. He goes around making sure there are no lights showing to guide enemy bombers towards us and so forth.'

'Well, he certainly guided my fist towards him. It's just a pity it had to connect with you. Say, that's a very sore-looking bruise. If it's any consolation, Captain, I've brought you a bottle of Bourbon and some Hershey bars for your men.'

He took from his sergeant several packages and placed them on my desk. 'We mustn't let this unfortunate beginning affect our future relations,' he went on. 'We've got to beat Hitler together, haven't we, old-timer?'

I could not help feeling a pulse of annoyance at this phrase 'old-timer' but then I felt Wilson's restraining touch on my arm and I relaxed again.

'Yes, of course,' I agreed. 'And, Colonel –'

' 'Ere, Napoleon, what's 'appened to my stirrup pump that was in the bicycle shed –' said Hodges angrily, entering without so much as a knock.

He broke off when he saw who was with me. For his part, the colonel turned and contemplated the new arrival coldly.

'Oh, hello, Colonel,' exclaimed Hodges in a fawning kind of voice while a false smile appeared on his ape-like face. 'I hope there's no hard feelings about the other night?'

'It seems to have been poor Captain Mainwaring here who bore the brunt of the hard feelings,' said Schultz meaningfully.

'Yeah, well – accidents 'appen, don't they?' stammered Hodges. Then he put out his hand. 'I just want you to know, Colonel, that in spite of what I said jokingly the other night, I'm proud to 'ave you and your men 'ere. Do

ESCAPED PRISONER OF WAR

THIS MAN IS DANGEROUS

NOTIFY YOUR NEAREST

JONES WONDERING GLUMLY WHICH OF HIS CUSTOMERS HAS SOUGHT REVENGE FOR A NIGGARDLY MEAT RATION BY PASTING HIS LIKENESS ONTO AN 'ESCAPED POW' POSTER.

you know, my own father spent twenty years of his life in America and 'e always said they were the best years he ever knew. That's right, a proper American patriot, 'e was and – and – although I've never myself been to God's own country, it's always been the land of my dreams.'

'Is that so?' asked the colonel and I could see, to my disgust, that he was beginning to warm towards Hodges. He even took the warden's hand and shook it. 'Oh well, I suppose we'd better let bygones be bygones.'

But this was simply more than I could stomach. Hodges' rudeness was the reason why I now bore an angry bruise on my face, the only wound, in fact, I had received in active service. And now it looked as if Hodges and the colonel were going to become friends. Was there any way to prevent it? Well, it may be instructive to the reader, as an indication of how valuable to the field commander is the power to make lightning decisions, to learn that in a trice a plan of action had formed in my mind.

'Alright then,' I said in a conciliatory voice. 'I think I'd better introduce you two properly. Mr Hodges, this is Colonel Schultz.'

'Pleased to meet you, Colonel Schultz,' said Hodges in a voice brimming over with false enthusiasm.

'Of course,' I went on, addressing the hypocritical warden, 'you may be a little surprised, Hodges, at the colonel's name.' I thereupon turned to the stocky American officer. 'Schultz? It's a German name, isn't it, sir?'

The colonel eyed me narrowly for a moment but I continued to smile pleasantly. Then he nodded. 'It was, certainly, when my grandfather brought it over from Germany seventy years ago.'

'Fascinating,' I said, as if I felt a keen interest in the subject. 'But I'll bet that Hodges here, as many other Englishmen would be, is probably a bit surprised to find that some of our allies have enemy names, aren't you, Hodges?'

The warden began to look unhappy. 'No, no – nothing like that –' he stammered.

'Really?' I asked. 'That's strange because I was certainly surprised when I first learned the colonel's name. I asked myself, I confess, if the fact that there are so many Germans in the American army might have had something to do with the Americans taking so long getting here. But then I decided that was unlikely.' I turned to the colonel. 'Nevertheless, Colonel Schultz, I should imagine you sometimes find it a bit hard to decide which side you should be fighting on, don't you?'

When the colonel replied, I recognised the same quiet, almost sad, note in his voice that had been in it the previous evening just before he had, as I believe the Americans put it, thrown a punch at Hodges.

'Not really, no,' he murmured. 'I've never had any trouble knowing the enemy.'

Since I had, a little mischievously I confess, 'set the whole thing up', I was on the alert and thus had plenty of time to duck. Normally I hate gratuitous violence but I must say I can't refrain from smiling as I write this at the recollection of the very satisfying thwack that the colonel's horny fist made as it connected with Hodges' cheek.

I will be brief in my concluding words. This is not from lack of either emotion or material. I could happily edit many more volumes concerning events in Walmington-on-Sea during the Second World War. But so many ties, both personal and professional, now bind me to Walmington that I might just run on and on like one of Frazer's gripping but interminable yarns. Far better to take my cue from Corporal Jones who, faced with my problem, might simply have snapped smartly to attention (very probably dropping his rifle and bayonet in the process) and requested: 'Permission to stop speaking, sir?'

Arthur Wilson

ARTHUR WILSON, MA

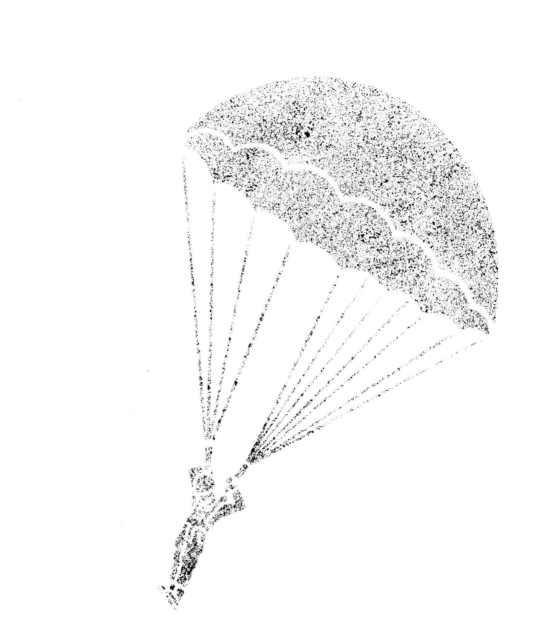